Mayo Clinic on Arthritis

SECOND EDITION
Completely Revised & Updated

Gene Hunder, M.D.

Editor in Chief

MASON CREST PUBLISHERS

Philadelphia, Pennsylvania

Mayo Clinic on Arthritis provides reliable, practical, easy-to-understand information on osteoarthritis and rheumatoid arthritis with a focus on self-help. Much of the information comes directly from the experience of Mayo Clinic physicians, nurses, research scientists, health educators, therapists and other health care professionals. This book supplements the advice of your personal physician, whom you should consult for individual medical problems. *Mayo Clinic on Arthritis* does not endorse any company or product. MAYO, MAYO CLINIC, MAYO CLINIC HEALTH INFORMATION and the Mayo triple-shield logo are marks of Mayo Foundation for Medical Education and Research.

© 2002 Mayo Foundation for Medical Education and Research

Hardcover Library Edition Published 2002
Mason Crest Publishers
370 Reed Road
Suite 302
Broomall, PA 19008-0914
(866) MCP-BOOK (toll free)

2 3 4 5 6 7 8 9 10

Library of Congress Cataloging-in-Publication Data on file at the Library of Congress

ISBN 1-59084-219-7

Printed in the United States of America

About arthritis

Arthritis is one of the most common health problems in the world. It's the No. 1 cause of disability in the United States. Nearly 40 million Americans have some form of arthritis. So if you have arthritis, you're not alone. Although a cure has yet to be found, effective treatments and other strategies are readily available.

This book focuses on the two most common forms of the disease — osteoarthritis and rheumatoid arthritis — but includes information useful to people with almost any form of the disease. Within these pages you'll find information you can put to use today to better manage your disease. Much of this information is what Mayo Clinic doctors, nurses and therapists use in caring for their patients.

If you understand your disease and treatment options and you put this knowledge to use in daily living, you can live more productively and comfortably, and you'll be able to communicate more effectively with your doctor and other health care professionals.

About Mayo Clinic

Mayo Clinic evolved from the frontier practice of Dr. William Worrall Mayo, and the partnership of his two sons, William J. and Charles H. Mayo, in the early 1900s. Pressed by the demands of their busy practice in Rochester, Minn., the Mayo brothers invited other physicians to join them, pioneering the private group practice of medicine. Today, with more than 2,000 physicians and scientists at its three major locations in Rochester, Minn., Jacksonville, Fla., and Scottsdale, Ariz., Mayo Clinic is dedicated to providing comprehensive diagnoses, accurate answers and effective treatments.

With this depth of medical knowledge, experience and expertise, Mayo Clinic occupies an unparalleled position as a health information resource. Since 1983, Mayo Clinic has published reliable health information for millions of consumers through award-winning newsletters, books and online services. Revenue from the publishing activities supports Mayo Clinic programs, including medical education and research.

Editorial staff

Editor in Chief
Gene Hunder, M.D.

Managing Editor
Richard Dietman

Editorial Research
Anthony Cook
Deirdre Herman
Michelle Hewlett

Proofreading
Miranda Attlesey
Donna Hanson

Contributing Writers
Felicia Busch
Michael Flynn
Linda Kephart Flynn
Lynn Madsen
D.R. Martin
Jeff Meade
Stephen Miller
Robin Silverman

Catherine Stroebel
Beth Watkins
Susan Wichmann

Illustration and Photography
Susan Balich
David Factor
Mary Frantz
John Hagen
Joseph Kane
Michael King
Richard Madsen
James Postier
Randy Ziegler

Creative Director
Daniel Brevick

Layout and Production
Craig King

Indexing
Larry Harrison

Contributing editors and reviewers

Olga Anderson, O.T.R.
Linda Arneson, R.P.T.
Brent Bauer, M.D.
Robert Beckenbaugh, M.D.
Jill Beed, J.D.
Tracy Berg, R.Ph.
Barbara Bruce, Ph.D.
Miguel Cabanela, M.D.
Kenneth Calamia, M.D.
Carl Chan, M.D.
Robert Cofield, M.D.
Marc Cohen, M.D.

Daniel Dogo-Esekie
Stephen Erickson, M.D.
Christopher Frye
Mary Jurisson, M.D.
Susan Lepore, O.T.R.
Ann Lund, O.T.R.
Harvinder Luthra, M.D.
Thomas Mason, M.D.
Eric Matteson, M.D.
Jennifer K. Nelson, R.D.
Terry Oh, M.D.
Christopher Sletten, Ph.D.

Preface

The second edition of *Mayo Clinic on Arthritis* was prepared with the same goal in mind as the first edition — to help you take control of your arthritis. In addition to the reliable information contained in the first edition, the second edition contains new information about the latest arthritis drugs, including biologic agents, as well as new information about surgical procedures and places to get support. A glossary has been added, and the chapter on complementary and alternative medicine has been updated.

Along with this new information, there are tips on managing your arthritis, including protecting your joints, exercise, pain control, diet and, equally important, how to maintain a positive attitude.

You'll also find information on potential new treatments of arthritis. There are practical tips on traveling with arthritis and on coping with it at work. This book concludes with a chapter that lists and describes other reliable sources of information on arthritis, including helpful recommendations for evaluating health information you find on the Web.

Mayo Clinic doctors who specialize in arthritis reviewed each chapter for accuracy. They were assisted by Mayo specialists in orthopedic surgery, physical therapy, psychiatry, occupational therapy, nutrition, pain management and human resources.

We can't promise a cure for arthritis, but we can tell you that your disease doesn't have to defeat you. Arthritis can be a disabling disease. Most often it isn't.

If you consistently apply the information in this book to your daily living, you'll live more productively and comfortably.

That's our commitment to you.

Gene Hunder, M.D.
Editor in Chief

Contents

Preface   v

Chapter 1 **Understanding arthritis**   1
    What causes arthritis?   2
    Common forms of arthritis   4
    Other arthritic disorders   10
    Related musculoskeletal conditions   14

Chapter 2 **Protecting your joints**   17
    Fundamentals of joint protection   18
    Using assistive devices   22
    Equipment resources   28

Chapter 3 **Exercising properly**   29
    Importance of exercise   29
    Tailoring your program   30
    Your activity goals   32
    Organized programs   32
    Assess your fitness   34
    Getting started   38
    Warning signs   39
    Recommended exercises   40

Chapter 4 **Tips on pain control**   51
    Treating pain at home   52
    Professional help for pain   54

Chapter 5 **Eating for better health**   59
    The basics   59
    Menu planning   63
    Cooking with ease   64
    Eating out   65
    Special nutrition issues   67

Chapter 6 **Your thoughts, feelings and beliefs and your health**   73
    The healer within   74
    Listening to your body   75

Accentuate the positive 76

Stress busting: Relaxation techniques 77

Seeking support: You're not alone 81

Simplifying your life 81

The rest is rest 83

You're in control 83

For more information 84

Chapter 7 **Medications for arthritis** 85

NSAIDs 86

COX-2 inhibitors 90

Corticosteroids 92

DMARDs 98

Immunosuppressants 102

Biologic agents 108

Pain reducers (analgesics) 111

Antidepressant drugs 113

Muscle relaxants 113

Tranquilizers 114

Visco supplementation 114

Arthritis medications guide 115

Chapter 8 **Surgical treatments** 121

Selecting a surgeon 121

Common forms of joint surgery 122

Which joints can surgery help? 124

Preparing for your surgery 131

Potential risks and complications 132

Your hospital stay 133

Rehabilitation 133

Recovery at home 134

Life after recovery 134

Chapter 9 **Complementary and alternative treatments** 135

Options available 136

Words of caution 143

How to evaluate complementary medicine 145

Make no assumptions 146

Chapter 10 **Promising trends in treatment**   147

Medications   148

Genes   150

Surgery   151

Lifestyle   152

Chapter 11 **Traveling with arthritis**   153

Planning your trip   154

Do you need a professional?   155

Booking a hotel   155

What to take along   156

Traveling by air   158

Traveling by train   158

Traveling by bus   159

Traveling by car   159

Traveling by ship   160

Touring overseas   160

Organizations that can help   162

Chapter 12 **On the job with arthritis**   165

Know your rights   166

Protect your joints   167

Be a smarter commuter   168

Make friends with your computer   169

Keep an open mind about your job and career   170

Finding a new job   172

Organizations that can help   177

Chapter 13 **Where to get more help**   179

The Arthritis Foundation   179

Mayo Clinic health information   180

Surfing the Web   180

Your local library   181

Bookstores   182

Words of caution   182

Glossary   185

Index   191

Chapter 1

Understanding arthritis

A rthritis is one of the most common medical problems in the world. It is the No. 1 cause of disability in the United States among adults age 65 and older. One person in seven, or nearly 40 million Americans, has some form of arthritis. As baby boomers age, the number of people with arthritis is expected to increase. By 2020, an estimated 59 million people will have the disease. The costs for medical care and lost productivity amount to an estimated $65 billion annually.

Arthritis affects people of all ages. Women are at special risk, accounting for almost two-thirds of people with arthritis.

The word *arthritis* is a blend of the Greek words *arthron*, for "joint," and *itis*, for "inflammation." So *arthritis* literally means "joint inflammation."

Although people often talk about arthritis as one disease, it's not. Arthritis occurs in more than 100 forms. Some forms occur gradually as a result of natural wear of joints, and others appear suddenly and then disappear, recurring at a later date regardless of treatment. Other forms are chronic and may be progressive.

Joint pain, stiffness and a sense of discomfort after periods of rest or inactivity are probably the best known general symptoms of arthritis. But arthritic disorders frequently affect more than joints alone. Some forms can affect other organs in your body and can even threaten your life. Fortunately, these potentially fatal forms are rare.

What causes arthritis?

Most of the underlying causes of arthritis are unclear. Physicians know that physical trauma, such as an ankle sprain or a knee injury, can set the stage for osteoarthritis, the most common form of arthritis. Other causes of arthritis are lack of physical activity, excessive weight and joint defects such as bowlegs. The aging process is a factor in osteoarthritis. That's why it's sometimes called wear-and-tear arthritis. Genetic diseases can cause weak cartilage, leading to excess cartilage wear.

Genetic factors are important in the cause of some other types of arthritis, such as rheumatoid arthritis and several other less common forms. In contrast to osteoarthritis, which is a disease of the cartilage, forms of arthritis associated with an abnormal immune system, such as rheumatoid arthritis, cause inflammation of the lining of the joint. Other possible causes or factors include the environment (food, water and air), infectious agents (viruses, bacteria or fungi) and an imbalance of certain enzymes. Stress or other forms of emotional trauma can worsen symptoms.

Although the underlying causes of arthritis are unclear, the effects are not. Arthritis in its various forms may be associated with the following:

- Breakdown of cartilage — occurs in osteoarthritis, rheumatoid arthritis and other forms of inflammatory arthritis, such as lupus
- Inflammation of the lining of the joint (synovial membrane), blood vessels, muscles, tendons and ligaments — occurs in inflammatory arthritis and other forms of arthritis in which inflammation spreads to other tissues of the body
- Development of crystals in the fluid of the joint (synovial fluid) — contributes to the development of attacks of acute gout and pseudogout
- Shortening or shrinkage of muscles or tendons, leading to joint deformities — occurs in any type of arthritis if the joint becomes immobilized
- Tightening of the skin — occurs mainly in scleroderma
- Damaged internal organs — can occur in rheumatoid arthritis and in other forms of inflammatory arthritis
- Loss of joint movement — occurs as a result of damage to a joint or weak muscles
- Decreased muscle strength — occurs if a joint is not moved for an extended period
- Decreased mobility — occurs as a result of long-term lack of exercise or joint damage; may be permanent

Anatomy of a joint

The joints in your body are made of materials designed to provide for a lifetime of service. Bones in your joints are capped with shock-absorbing cartilage. Cartilage is a tough, smooth, slippery material that prevents bone-against-bone contact.

The joint is surrounded and lubricated by the synovial membrane, which forms and releases a fluid. The synovial membrane is the inner lining of the joint capsule. The joint capsule is a tough, fibrous material that attaches to bone on either side of the joint. It helps stabilize the joint. Ligaments are shorter cords of strong fiber that attach bone to bone and provide joint alignment and support.

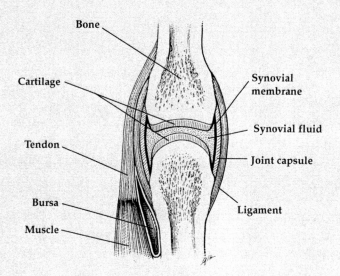

The joint is held firmly together by muscles tipped by tendons that attach to bone just outside the capsule above or below the joint. Friction-reducing bursae — small fluid-filled sacs between muscles or between muscles, tendons and bone — are present near some joints. Synovial membranes line the inside of each bursa and also release a lubricating fluid.

And that's it. The design is simple and the materials are durable. Some people reach age 100 without a hint of joint pain. They are, however, the exception.

Common forms of arthritis

The vast majority of people with arthritis have one of two forms — osteoarthritis or rheumatoid arthritis.

Osteoarthritis

Osteoarthritis, sometimes called degenerative arthritis, degenerative joint disease or osteoarthrosis, makes up about half of the kinds of arthritis. It affects nearly 21 million Americans and is most common in women. It may affect any joint in your body. Initially it tends to occur in only one joint. But if your fingers are affected, multiple hand joints may become arthritic.

With osteoarthritis, the problem lies in the cartilage that cushions the ends of bones of your joints. Over time, the cartilage deteriorates and its smooth surface roughens. Eventually, if the cartilage wears down completely, you may be left with bone rubbing on bone, and the ends of your bones become damaged. This is often painful.

Some scientists believe the cartilage damage may be due to an imbalance of enzymes released from the cartilage cells or from the lining of the joint. When balanced, these enzymes allow for the natural breakdown and regeneration of cartilage. But too much of the enzymes can cause the joint cartilage to break down faster than it's rebuilt. The exact cause of this enzyme imbalance is unclear.

Severe injury to one or more joints at an early age also may lead to osteoarthritis years later. Similarly, excessive stressful use of joints over years may cause osteoarthritis in those joints later on.

Your body attempts to repair the damage, but the repairs may be inadequate, resulting instead in growth of new bone along the sides of the existing bone, which produces prominent lumps, most often on the hands and feet. Each of the steps in this repair process produces pain. The pain and tenderness over the bony lumps may be most marked early in the course of the disease and less evident later on.

If you live long enough, you'll most likely experience one or more painful joints, because osteoarthritis affects almost everyone with age. Osteoarthritis most often develops after age 45. In young people, in the absence of a joint injury, osteoarthritis is relatively rare. Those who are affected often have a family history of the disease.

Although an active lifestyle may slow the process, almost all Americans older than 60 have mild symptoms of osteoarthritis in the

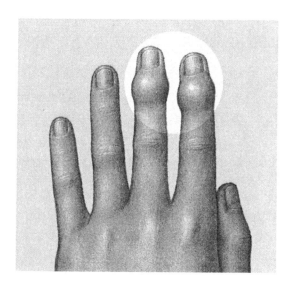

Heberden's nodes are bony lumps at the ends of fingers with osteoarthritis. Initially painful, they are mostly a cosmetic concern once the pain subsides.

neck or spine. Many older adults have osteoarthritis but don't know it until their doctor sees it on a routine X-ray.

If you have osteoarthritis, you may experience:

- Pain in a joint during or after use
- Discomfort in a joint before or during a change in the weather
- Swelling and stiffness in a joint, particularly after using it
- Bony lumps on the middle or end joints of your fingers or the base of your thumb
- Loss of flexibility of a joint

Osteoarthritis commonly occurs in the neck or back. Disks between vertebrae are made of cartilage. These disks can wear out. When this happens, the spaces between the bones narrow. Bony outgrowths, called spurs (osteophytes), frequently form. When bone surfaces rub together, the joint and areas around the cartilage become inflamed and painful.

Gradually, your spine stiffens and loses flexibility. If several disks are involved, you may lose height.

Spinal stenosis is a condition associated with osteoarthritis of the spine. Spinal stenosis occurs when degenerating disks and spurs bulge into the spinal canal and compress the spinal cord or nerve roots where they exit the spine between the vertebrae.

Osteoarthritis also frequently affects the hips and knees because they bear most of your weight. You can have chronic pain or varying amounts of discomfort when you stand and walk. Swelling also may occur, especially in your knees.

The hands and feet also are often involved in osteoarthritis. In the hands, the fingertip (distal) joints and those next to them (proximal finger joints) tend to be affected. The joint at the base of the thumb also is a common site for osteoarthritis to develop. In the feet, the bunion joint — where the big toe attaches to the foot — is the most frequent location of osteoarthritis. The joint becomes larger with bony swelling and less flexible and may make wearing shoes uncomfortable and walking painful. As the arthritis progresses, the hand and foot joints may be painful, and they may sting and ache out of proportion to what you might expect. The joints may be quite tender and even show some redness early on. Eventually, the acute discomfort lessens. Some redness and soft tissue swelling can occur. The swelled tissue becomes bony.

Osteoarthritis often affects joints on just one side of the body (asymmetric), especially early in its course. Gradually, joints on the opposite side of your body may become affected.

Although it generally isn't a seriously disabling condition, osteoarthritis won't go away. The acute pain of early osteoarthritis often tends to fade within a year of its appearance, but it may return if you overuse the affected joint. Still, unless multiple joints are involved, the effects of osteoarthritis are unlikely to be disabling physically. And keeping fit helps prevent disability.

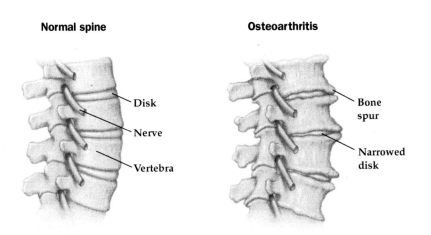

Normal spine   **Osteoarthritis**

Disk

Nerve

Vertebra

Bone spur

Narrowed disk

Elastic structures called disks cushion vertebrae in a normal spine, keeping it flexible. In osteoarthritis, disks may narrow and spurs form. Pain and stiffness may occur where bone surfaces rub together.

If a complete breakdown of cartilage occurs, the ends of the bones rub together and eventually become polished in a process called eburnation. At this advanced stage, it's difficult to use the joint.

If you think you may have osteoarthritis, schedule an appointment with your doctor. Pain with the use of one or more joints is a key to the diagnosis of osteoarthritis. Bone spurs and wearing down of cartilage may be evident in an X-ray of the affected joint, indicating the presence of osteoarthritis. The fact that osteoarthritis is so common is another clue that could explain your joint pain. Magnetic resonance imaging (MRI) may show early changes in joints involved, but is usually not indicated.

Changes of osteoarthritis occur in the cartilage before they are evident on an X-ray. Consequently, X-ray findings may be normal early on.

There is no blood test for osteoarthritis, but some blood tests and the appearance of the X-ray can help exclude rheumatoid and other forms of arthritis. The nature of the joint pain and the specific joints affected also help to distinguish these forms of arthritis.

Remember, the presence of osteoarthritis does not, in itself, indicate a problem. Many people have no symptoms or disability from their arthritis. Many are unaware they have osteoarthritis and have no apparent discomfort.

Rheumatoid arthritis

Unlike osteoarthritis, rheumatoid arthritis isn't associated with the wear and tear of use or with an injury. The disease can strike at any time, but most often it develops between ages 20 and 50 years. An estimated 2 million Americans have rheumatoid arthritis, and roughly twice as many women as men are affected.

Rheumatoid arthritis is probably an autoimmune disease. That's a disease in which your immune system attacks your body. Researchers suspect that an as yet unidentified agent, possibly a virus or form of bacteria, stimulates the immune system to attack the invading agent. In autoimmune diseases, the cells usually engaged in fighting the invader become confused and instead attack your joints.

The principal area of attack of rheumatoid arthritis is the lining of the joint. When you have rheumatoid arthritis, white blood cells — whose normal job is to attack unwanted invaders — move from your bloodstream into your synovial membrane. There, the blood cells appear to cause the membrane to become inflamed.

The inflammation results in a thickening of the synovial membrane and a release of chemicals from synovial membrane cells and blood cells

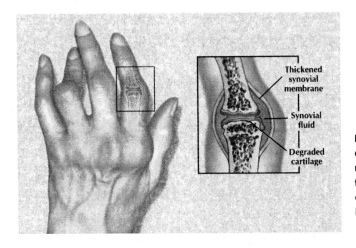

Thickened
synovial
membrane

Synovial
fluid

Degraded
cartilage

**Rheumatoid arthritis
often leads to defor-
mity in fingers. During
flare-ups of the dis-
ease, your hand may
be painful and weak.**

that have entered the membrane. If the inflammation persists, the released chemicals begin to destroy cartilage, bone, tendons and ligaments in the joint.

Gradually, the joint loses its shape and alignment. Ligaments, muscle and bone weaken. This weakening may lead to looseness in the joint. Eventually, the joint may be destroyed.

Rheumatoid arthritis often is more disabling than osteoarthritis. Painful, deformed joints may lead to loss of mobility and stability. Joints affected will be swollen, painful, tender and warm during the initial attack and during flare-ups that may follow.

Signs and symptoms of rheumatoid arthritis can include:
- Pain and swelling in the smaller joints of your hands and feet
- Aching or stiffness of the joints and muscles, especially after you sleep or after periods of rest
- Loss of motion of the affected joints
- Loss of strength in muscles attached to the affected joints
- Deformity of the joints as time goes on
- Fatigue (severe during a flare-up)

Even if stricken with a severe form of rheumatoid arthritis, you'll probably retain flexibility in many joints. You may have less pain than the appearance of your deformed joints suggests.

Joints often affected by rheumatoid arthritis are those in your wrists, hands, feet and ankles. The disease can also involve your elbows, shoulders, hips, knees, neck and jaw. It generally affects joints on both sides of the body at the same time, for example, the knuckles of both hands. The most frequently involved joints are those of the hands and feet.

In rheumatoid arthritis, other sings and symptoms can occur outside the joints. In contrast to osteoarthritis, which affects only your bones and muscles, rheumatoid arthritis can affect your whole body, including such organs as your heart, blood vessels, lungs and eyes. Rheumatoid arthritis causes problems in many joints at the same time, but osteoarthritis usually causes symptoms in only one or a few joints, even though several joints may be affected.

Small lumps, called rheumatoid nodules, may form under the skin of your elbows, hands, knees, toes and the back of your scalp. These nodules, usually painless, range in size from that of a pea to a walnut.

If you have persistent discomfort and swelling in multiple joints on both sides of your body, your doctor may order one or more of the following blood tests:

Erythrocyte sedimentation rate test. Sometimes referred to as your sed rate, this blood test determines the rate at which your red blood cells settle to the bottom of a tube. Cells that settle faster than normal indicate the presence of inflammation, which is typical of active rheumatoid arthritis. With osteoarthritis, your sedimentation rate tends to be normal.

C-reactive protein test. C-reactive proteins are chemical substances that are generally produced within 1 to 2 days of the onset of inflammation. A C-reactive protein (CRP) test measures the level of such proteins in your blood. In people with rheumatoid arthritis, their CRP level is typically elevated. The CRP test is highly sensitive and generally more accurate in diagnosing active rheumatoid arthritis than the traditional sed rate test. The erythrocyte sedimentation rate and CRP tests are often used to help monitor the degree of inflammation of rheumatoid arthritis.

Rheumatoid factor test. This test is used to identify an antibody in your blood called rheumatoid factor (RF). Four out of five people with rheumatoid arthritis have this abnormal antibody, which typically isn't present in people with osteoarthritis. It appears to be a marker of the disease and not a cause of arthritis symptoms. Rheumatoid factor is also present in some people with other diseases, such as chronic infections, so it isn't specific to rheumatoid arthritis.

In addition to blood tests, a diagnosis of rheumatoid arthritis often includes X-ray examinations to look for damage to affected joints. Because it often takes several months of active inflammation before damage appears on an X-ray, your doctor may not order X-rays if your symptoms have just developed. A sequence of X-rays obtained over time can show the progression of rheumatoid arthritis.

Often, rheumatoid arthritis is chronic, although it tends to vary in severity and may even come and go. Periods of increased disease activity, called flare-ups or flares, alternate with periods of relative remission, during which the swelling, pain, difficulty in sleeping and weakness fade or disappear.

When first diagnosed, it's impossible to predict how severe your rheumatoid arthritis may eventually be. If you have fairly continuous symptoms for 4 or 5 years, your condition is more likely to pose a lifetime challenge. Periodic examination of your joints and tests such as the sed rate can be done to monitor your rheumatoid arthritis. After 10 or 20 years, the symptoms of inflammation, especially joint swelling, may stabilize, but joint deformities and some pain remain.

There's no cure for rheumatoid arthritis, but with proper treatment, a strategy of joint protection and changes in lifestyle, most people live long, productive lives after their arthritis develops. As with osteoarthritis, both professional care and self-care are essential. Starting early in the disease on a carefully planned, individualized treatment program outlined by your physician and other health care professionals offers the best chance of reducing the impact of the disease on your lifestyle.

Other arthritic disorders

In addition to osteoarthritis and rheumatoid arthritis, more than 100 conditions exist that doctors consider forms of arthritis. Various common sprains and strains — tennis elbow, bursitis, ankle sprain, frozen shoulder, carpal tunnel syndrome, even heel and back pain — are included in this category.

People who have arthritis are more prone to sprains and strains of tendons and ligaments, so it's important to be aware of this risk and to modify or even eliminate physical activities that place you at risk. Swimming, for example, is an excellent alternative to a sport such as soccer or touch football.

Although sprains and strains can be temporarily painful and disabling, they generally heal nicely without the need for extended or complicated medical treatments. In contrast, some uncommon arthritic conditions, left untreated, can pose a serious hazard to your health and can even threaten your life. Some of these rare forms involve the body in a widespread manner, affecting multiple organs and even blood vessels.

Here's a sampling of less common arthritic disorders, including some that pose a more serious threat to your health:

Lupus erythematosus (er-uh-them-uh-TO-sus)

This is an inflammatory disease occurring most often in women. It can affect the synovial membranes of all joints and cause a rash. At other times, different organs of your body become inflamed, such as your lungs, kidneys and blood vessels. Signs and symptoms may come and go with apparent triggers or patterns. Sometimes it's called systemic lupus erythematosus.

Anti-nuclear antibodies are proteins that react with nuclei of your body's cells. They are found in the blood of nearly all people with lupus erythematosus. Testing for anti-nuclear antibodies helps in the diagnosis of this disease. However, people with other autoimmune diseases may also have a positive result, so this test is not specific for lupus erythematosus.

Scleroderma (sklere-o-DER-muh)

A general tightening of the skin of your arms, face or hands, puffy hands and feet, and joint stiffness and pain may signal scleroderma. It's associated with an increase in fibrous tissue deposits in your skin. Although rare, the deposits can become more extensive internally, affecting virtually every organ in your body.

Scleroderma and lupus are occasionally called connective tissue diseases. People with scleroderma often also have Raynaud's phenomenon. With Raynaud's phenomenon, spasms of blood vessels in your hands and feet result in recurrent color changes in your skin. These changes are typically brought on by exposure to cold or stress.

Sjogren's (SHOW-grinz) syndrome

Although mild decreases in saliva and tears can be normal with aging, in this condition your tear and saliva glands become inflamed, which markedly interferes with the flow of tears and saliva. The result is dryness in your mouth and a sandy, gritty feeling in your eyes. Sjogren's syndrome may accompany rheumatoid arthritis, lupus, scleroderma or polymyositis. Middle-age women with these other forms of arthritis are at highest risk of Sjogren's syndrome.

Polymyositis (pol-e-mi-o-SI-tis)

This serious condition can cause inflammation and weakness of virtually all of the muscles of your body and throat and can make movement and swallowing difficult. It can also lead to lung problems.

Psoriatic (suh-re-AT-ik) arthritis

Your hand and foot joints are especially at risk in psoriatic arthritis, which is associated with psoriasis, a common skin disease. The synovial membrane becomes inflamed. The disease also affects tendons where they attach to bone.

Spondylarthropathy (spon-dil-ahr-THROP-uh-the)

If you have an inflammation of spinal joints and tendons and ligaments where they attach to bones in your spine, you may have a spondylarthropathy. This category of arthritis includes ankylosing spondylitis (ANK-kuh-loe-zing spon-duh-LI-tis), reactive arthritis (Reiter's syndrome), and arthritis with chronic inflammation of the intestines. Ankylosing spondylitis usually occurs in men and begins before age 40. It may result in a stiff ("poker" or "bamboo") spine.

As with ankylosing spondylitis, reactive arthritis (Reiter's syndrome) involves inflammation of tendons and ligaments where they attach to the bones as well as the joints. But here the problem lies more in joints in your arms or legs than in your spine. In addition to joint pain, you may have heel pain, a urinary tract discharge, a painful inflammation of your eyes and a rash.

Gout

Gout generally attacks older men and can come on suddenly, resulting in intense pain and swelling in a single joint of your foot, often at the base of the big toe. An excessive concentration of uric acid in your body can cause microscopic crystals to form in the fluids that lubricate the affected joint. A painful inflammation occurs as your body tries to rid itself of the crystals. Diagnosis can be made by identifying crystals in fluid drawn (aspirated) from an inflamed joint.

Pseudogout (SOO-doe-gout)

In pseudogout, calcium salt crystals build up in the joint cartilage and are released into the joint cavity, causing pain and swelling similar to gout. But the affected joint is more likely to be your knee, wrist or ankle.

Polymyalgia rheumatica (pol-ee-my-AL-juh roo-MA-ti-kuh)

This arthritis most commonly affects white adults beyond age 50. It's characterized by pain and stiffness in the muscles of your shoulders, neck, upper arms, lower back, thighs and hips. A slight fever, fatigue and unexplained weight loss also may occur. The typical course is often about 2 years, after which polymyalgia rheumatica usually disappears. It may progress into giant cell arteritis. The erythrocyte sedimentation rate is usually very high.

Giant cell arteritis (ahr-tuh-RI-tis)

If you develop new headaches and the arteries on the sides of your head near your eyes (temporal arteries) are thickened and tender, you may have giant cell arteritis (inflammation in the arteries). Left untreated, narrowed or blocked arteries in giant cell arteritis can lead to partial or total blindness or other serious vascular problems, such as a stroke. Giant cell arteritis is also known as temporal arteritis or cranial arteritis. It occurs only after age 50. Prompt diagnosis and treatment with prednisone can prevent vascular complications.

Polyarteritis nodosa (pol-e-ahr-tuh-RI-tis no-DO-suh)

Polyarteritis nodosa is an inflammation of blood vessels, especially arteries. It's a potentially fatal disorder that can affect or even block multiple arteries throughout your body, reducing the supply of blood to vital organs, including your heart.

Bursitis

A bursa is a sac-like cavity located at places in body tissues where friction would otherwise develop. These bursae may become inflamed by trauma, by excess use of overlying tissues or as part of a number of forms of arthritis. This results in bursitis.

Tendinitis

Tendons are fibrous cords that connect your muscles to your bones and other structures within your body. Inflammation may develop with use or in conjunction with arthritis.

Arthritic infections

Your joints can become infected by any germ entering your blood. If, for example, a boil or other infection releases the staphylococcal bacteria into your blood, these bacteria can spread to a knee or some other joint. The pain is usually intense and sudden.

Gonorrhea, a sexually transmitted bacterial disease, can cause painful joints and a rash.

Lyme disease can lead to arthritis. After a tick bite, a red or pink disk-shaped rash may appear, followed by fever, chills, sore throat, fatigue and nausea. Weeks later, stiffness and pain may occur in your joints.

If you have tuberculosis, you are at risk of a form of infectious arthritis called tuberculous arthritis. Hepatitis B, German measles (rubella), mumps and other diseases caused by viruses also can lead to arthritis.

Related musculoskeletal conditions

Fibromyalgia

Fibromyalgia is a disorder that affects your muscles, tendons and ligaments. It differs from arthritis in that the pain is in nearby joint tissues instead of in the joints themselves. In addition, unlike arthritis, fibromyalgia doesn't cause inflammation — just pain.

The main symptom of fibromyalgia is an "aching all over." The pain may be a deep ache or burning sensation. Other symptoms associated with fibromyalgia may include:

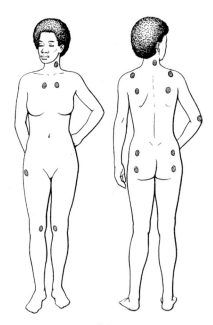

- Chronic fatigue
- Difficulty sleeping
- Stiffness
- Headaches
- Pain during menstruation
- Digestive problems
- Numbness
- Tingling
- Sensitivity to weather and temperature changes

Because its symptoms are many and varied and they don't follow a consistent pattern, fibromyalgia is often called fibromyalgia syndrome.

Common locations of painful aching associated with fibromyalgia

Most often, symptoms of fibromyalgia first become noticeable in your 30s. They may flare and then subside, but they usually don't disappear completely. Although fibromyalgia tends to stay with you, it isn't progressive, disabling or life-threatening.

Doctors aren't sure what causes this condition. One theory is that certain factors, such as stress, poor sleep, physical or emotional trauma, or being out of shape, may trigger the condition in people who are more sensitive to pain. Numerous other possibilities as to its cause are under study.

Doctors generally diagnose fibromyalgia only after they've tested and eliminated other conditions.

Osteoporosis

Unlike osteo*arthritis*, which is caused by a breakdown of cartilage within joints, osteo*porosis* is a bone-weakening disease. It's caused by a gradual loss of calcium from bones, making them thinner and weaker and more prone to fracture. Also in contrast to osteoarthritis, which causes stiffness and pain, osteoporosis is symptomless at first. A bone fracture may be the first indication there's a problem. Like osteoarthritis, osteoporosis is common and associated with aging, occurring in women most commonly after menopause. Most of the pain associated with osteoporosis is caused by fractures.

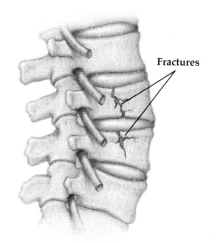

Fractures

When osteoporosis occurs, vertebrae may become compressed and fractured as a result of weakness in bone structure.

It's possible to go on with descriptions of increasingly uncommon forms of arthritis, but that's not what this book is about.

This book is about health and hope. It's about dealing with the pain, inflammation and limitations that may accompany osteoarthritis and rheumatoid arthritis. It's about getting on with your life despite aches and pains and the joint problems these forms of arthritis cause.

The good news is that these two most common forms of arthritis aren't life-threatening and do respond to medical treatments and self-care. You need knowledge about your arthritis, your limitations, your treatment options and, most importantly, the self-help steps you can take to control your arthritis in partnership with your physician.

Armed with this information and a positive attitude, you can move forward, adjusting your lifestyle where necessary without compromising your happiness and fulfillment.

Chapter 2

Protecting your joints

Y ou wouldn't deliberately drive your automobile into a pothole or over a speed bump at 55 miles an hour. Doing either could damage your car and shorten its useful life. Neither would you go out of your way to injure your joints, especially if you have arthritis. They may be stiff and painful already, and injury would limit them — and you — even more. The goal of this chapter is to help you protect your joints from harm.

One of the most effective ways to preserve and protect your joints is exercise. Although it might seem as if exercise will increase your risk of injury, proper exercise can actually extend the life of your joints. Exercise can:

- Strengthen muscles surrounding your arthritic joints, providing them with much-needed support
- Increase your joint flexibility and range of motion
- Reduce fatigue, a major issue, especially among people with rheumatoid arthritis
- Boost your energy levels
- Help you lose weight, thereby reducing the load on your joints
- Contribute to the quality of your sleep

Exercise is discussed at length in depth in Chapter 3. But before you embark on a plan for physical activity, here are some basic principles of joint protection.

Fundamentals of joint protection

Seek medical advice

If you're not accustomed to physical activity, and especially if you're uncertain what kind of activity would be most beneficial or appropriate, check with your doctor. He or she might refer you to an occupational or physical therapist.

Start slowly

To maintain motion without damaging your joints, move each joint through its full pain-free range of motion at least once daily. Range-of-motion exercise also provides nutrition to cartilage. This pain-free range may vary from day to day. Take care not to overdo it, especially if you have rheumatoid arthritis.

Gently stretch muscles of affected joints at least once a day, perhaps in the morning when you get up and definitely at the beginning and end of any exercise. Stretching loosens your muscles and reduces the risk of injury. Slow and gentle stretching can also increase a stiff joint's range of motion. Sudden jerking or bouncing may be harmful to your joints, so aim for slow, fluid stretching motions.

Warm up and cool down

You can also warm up joints and muscles with a heating pad or hot pack, with massage or by gently walking in place for a few minutes. A warm bath or shower before you exercise also might help. Hot packs, applied for 20 minutes, should feel warm and soothing but not hot. Because heat could increase swelling and pain, it's important not to apply it to an already warm, swollen joint. After exercise, you may apply cold to the affected joints for 10 to 15 minutes.

Step up the pace gradually

Start at a comfortable level. That might be a walk to the end of your driveway and back. If that's what you can do, start with that. Once you're reasonably comfortable, increase the distance a little at a time.

Try exercising at different times of the day. Find the time when you feel the least pain and stiffness.

Learn to understand and respect your pain

Learn to tell the difference between the general discomfort of arthritis

Trim those extra pounds

If you weigh more than you should, you have lots of company. Most Americans fall into this category. But also keep this fact in mind: being seriously overweight has significant implications for your health.

If you exceed your optimal weight, you're more likely to develop osteoarthritis of the knee. And if you already have this common problem, those extra pounds can speed the breakdown of cartilage in your knee joints, leading to pain and disability. Other arthritic joints, including your back, hips, ankles, big toes and hands can also be damaged by extra weight.

Of course, many factors may contribute to the development of arthritis. One is heredity. Another is an injury to the joint. Still another is simply the passage of time. But if you're overweight, those extra pounds can accelerate the process.

Extra pounds are also a major risk factor for diabetes and cardio-vascular disease. Losing even a few pounds — a 5 percent to 10 percent weight loss — can reduce risk factors for cardiovascular disease, such as high blood pressure and increased blood cholesterol, and lower your chances for knee pain and disability.

Good nutrition and proper exercise are keys to weight control. For tips on exercise and nutrition, see Chapters 3 and 5.

and pain from overuse of a joint. Adjust your activity level or method of doing a task to avoid excessive pain. Be aware that you're more likely to damage your joints when they are painful and swollen. Don't overexercise tender, injured or badly inflamed joints.

Pain is considered excessive if it alters your breathing pattern and you find that you're holding your breath or breathing more rapidly than normal. Excessive pain is pain from which you can't be distracted or that does not readily reduce in intensity when you stop exercising.

If increased pain lasts more than an hour or two after exercise or pain comes on more quickly day after day, chances are you're doing too much or doing inappropriate exercise.

Know your limits

If you have osteoarthritis of the hip or knee and the bones and cartilage of the affected joint aren't too worn down, then a low-impact activity such as walking might be just what you need. But if the bones and cartilage are significantly worn down, walking could cause even more damage. Non-weight-bearing activity, such as swimming or riding a stationary bike, may be a better choice.

If you have rheumatoid arthritis, low-impact activities are best, depending on the amount of wear and tear on joints affected by the arthritis. If the joint in question is not painful and a particular activity doesn't seem to cause pain, it's probably OK to proceed. But if the activity causes pain, stop and consider an alternative exercise.

Remember to rest

The concept can be confusing. First your doctor may tell you to stay active. Then you may hear about the special importance of rest.

It's a delicate balance. At times, you'll need to rest to save energy. At other times, you'll need to exercise to maintain the strength of your muscles, nourish your joints, stay reasonably flexible and build your stores of energy.

There are two forms of rest: joint rest and whole-body rest. It's important to obtain both.

Joint rest. When joints are injured or badly inflamed, they need to rest and may require immobilization with splints. The joints may be gradually mobilized when the acute problem is resolved. Using an affected joint helps keep it healthy and promotes the supply of nutrients and oxygen

If you have arthritis in your hands, there are right and wrong ways to hold a book. A pinching grip (left) strains your finger joints and may cause pain. Rest your book comfortably on your palms (right) to ease pain.

to the joint. Even so, individual joints can become fatigued after periods of exertion. So if your hip muscles seem tired during the day, that's a good signal to sit down and rest.

Whole-body rest. If you have arthritis, and especially if you have rheumatoid arthritis, a well-rested body is an important goal to achieve on a daily basis. Your rheumatoid arthritis makes you especially vulnerable to fatigue because many of your joints may be inflamed. In addition, inflammation may be present in organs of your body. Your condition can also cause anemia, which contributes to your fatigue.

Fatigue associated with arthritis is a deep-down exhaustion, often including muscle weakness. It can make virtually everything you attempt to do seem like too great an effort. It can leave you feeling almost helpless. You may begin to wonder if you have any control over your life.

The process of inflammation can cause pain that may bring on fatigue. If you experience a period of joint inflammation (flare), you need to schedule more time to rest your joints throughout the day. Joint pain might also cause you to change positions periodically to take weight off the affected joints. Pain can also cause you to lose sleep or prevent you from sleeping well.

If you're exhausted, you may not feel like doing much. But if you don't engage in enough physical activity, your muscles will only get weaker and you'll find it even more difficult to get started with physical activity.

Alternatively, maybe you tend to keep on working until a job is done, regardless of discomfort — whether walking to the corner and back or finishing the laundry. That strategy might not be the best either. If you exercise too strenuously or too often without taking a break, you can strain muscles and joints and risk injury.

The key is to rest before you become too tired. Pace yourself. Don't work through those tired periods. Divide exercise or work activities into short segments with frequent breaks. Plan 10 minutes of rest every hour during periods of physical exertion. On the surface, that approach may sound disruptive and unreasonable, but it works.

From time to time during each day, find a comfortable position and relax for a while. An easy chair, a couch, a bed or a reclined seat in your parked vehicle are all potential options. You don't need to sleep, but you do need to give your body a break.

When it's bedtime, go to bed. Avoid the temptations of watching the

Devices to support and protect joints

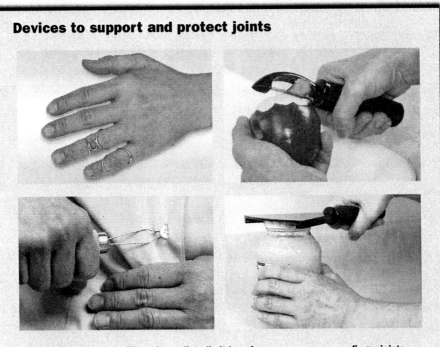

Clockwise from top left: Silver ring splints limit how far you can move your finger joints. They're less cumbersome than a traditional splint, so you can wear several on the same hand. A peeler with a thick rubber handle minimizes gripping action. A specially designed jar opener reduces twisting force to a slight turn. A thin wire hook helps you grasp a button and pull it through the buttonhole.

late news on TV or finishing a book chapter. A good night's sleep will give your joints the rest they need. It can also help restore your energy and enable you to deal more effectively with pain.

If you have rheumatoid arthritis, set a goal of 8 or 9 hours of sleep each night. If you have trouble sleeping, talk to your doctor about it promptly. When sleep disturbances are treated, fatigue usually improves.

Using assistive devices

Observing the basic principles of joint protection can help you extend the life of your joints. But even if you do your best to preserve your joints and reduce wear and tear, the basic measures may be insufficient. A painful knee may need a brace for support. Or you might opt for a cane to take weight off the joint as you walk. If your hands are affected, various helpful tools and gadgets are readily available to help you maintain your lifestyle.

People sometimes avoid assistive devices, believing they don't need the help or thinking that the use of special measures is a form of surrender. Some people believe an assistive device such as a cane will make them look old or may lead to loss of function. In reality, assistive devices allow you to be more independent with daily tasks, and in so doing, play an important role in self-management of arthritis.

Think about this: Few people think twice about getting into an automobile for a drive across town. But a car, in reality, is an assistive device. It makes it easier to accomplish a goal — in this case, to get from one place to another quicker and more comfortably.

Assistive devices do much the same thing. They're a means to an end. They make it easier for you to perform everyday activities, such as opening a stubborn jar or taking a shower.

Medical supply houses and catalogs offer various items. Most of them are inexpensive and affordable.

Sometimes, a little creativity is all you need. You can use plastic foam tubing, the kind used to insulate plumbing pipes in homes, to make tools and utensils easier to grasp. The insulation is available in different sizes and can be cut to fit all kinds of hand-held devices. The foam insulation also reduces vibration.

Selection of the right assistive device can minimize joint stress. Here are tips on using some of the many options available to you:

Hand aids

Look for aids that offer a wide-diameter grip. Most toothbrushes, for example, have thin handles that force you to grasp them with a tightly closed fist. If you have arthritis, this position can put painful stress on the joints and other structures of your fingers, thumb and wrist.

If you have arthritis in your hands, avoid making a tight fist or tightly pinching any object. A less physically stressful position for your hand is one in which your fingers and thumb are not tightly closed.

Grooming and personal hygiene

If you have limited range of motion, you might want to opt for long-handled brushes and combs. Bathing aids such as long-handled sponges and brushes can help you reach your feet and other parts of your body with less effort and pain. Use an electric toothbrush, a Radius toothbrush or one with a foam handle. Use mirrors with foam rubber handles for an easier grasp. Bath benches, grab bars and toilet seat risers can help you bathe and take care of your personal hygiene with greater ease, safety and independence.

Getting dressed

If you have trouble reaching your feet, buy a shoehorn with an extension handle. Shop around for a stocking aid that enables you to pull on hosiery without having to bend over. Look for tools that grip buttons and zippers. Sew elasticized Velcro tabs onto shirt cuffs to allow the cuff to stretch as you slip your hand through or sew cuff buttons on with elasticized thread.

Select wraparound skirts or stretch trousers if limited range of motion makes dressing a challenge. Clip-on neckties are convenient, or with a regular necktie, leave the knot tied and slip the tie over your head.

In the kitchen

Organize your work area. Make sure everything you use often is easy to reach. Store frequently used cookware and utensils in cabinets at hip-to-shoulder height. Eliminate things you seldom use.

A single-lever faucet in your kitchen sink can make the numerous tasks you perform at the sink a little less taxing on your finger joints.

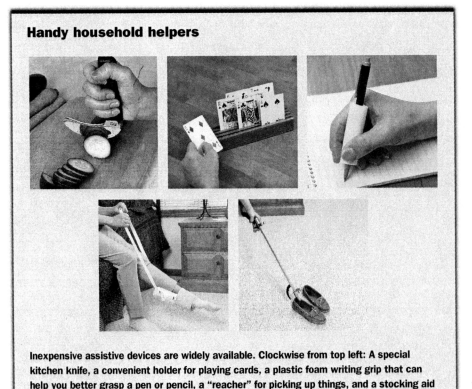

Handy household helpers

Inexpensive assistive devices are widely available. Clockwise from top left: A special kitchen knife, a convenient holder for playing cards, a plastic foam writing grip that can help you better grasp a pen or pencil, a "reacher" for picking up things, and a stocking aid that enables you to put on socks or stockings without bending down.

An electric can opener is easier to operate than a manual opener. The same is true for carving knives. An electric knife can make some kitchen work go more smoothly. Buy a cutting board that features tiny raised spikes to hold foods firmly in place while you cut them. If you use a non-electric knife, buy one that's L-shaped with a wide-diameter vertical handle. To use this type of knife, grasp it like a dagger and use a sawing motion without applying much pressure.

In the grocery store, select prepared foods that don't require slicing and dicing. Chopped nuts, for example, cost a little more and but save you time and effort.

Buy a jar opener that can be mounted under a kitchen cabinet or counter.

Cleaning your home

For housework, use a long-handled mop, dustpan and broom. A sponge can enable you to use an open hand when washing windows. Keep cleaning supplies on each floor. Store supplies within easy reach.

If you have a front-loading clothes washer or dryer, consider placing it on wooden blocks for easier access. Avoid unnecessary bending or stooping.

In the shop

For some activities, there's no alternative for a manual tool. But in many cases, there's a powered alternative. For example, power nail drivers are preferable to hammers. Power screwdrivers are easier on your joints than conventional screwdrivers.

Using a brace

Along with devices designed to help you perform specific chores, you might need to give a painful joint external support with a brace. Any brace, and especially a knee brace, should fit properly. It's important to work with your doctor and physical therapist to get a good fit.

Think of a brace as a splint you can remove. Both pain and swelling can be helped by immobilizing a joint. But remember, a brace doesn't offer a long-term solution to the problem of pain. A brace is good for only short-term relief. Long-term use of a brace may lead to weakened muscles and increased pain.

Using a cane

A cane that's fitted to your body and needs can provide welcome support and increase your independence. However, a poorly fitted cane may increase your problems.

Be kind to your joints every day

An important part of joint protection is simply avoiding situations that aggravate your condition. But how do you put that advice into practice in your daily life? Try these tips:

- When writing, use good posture and lighting. Relax your hand and neck often. If holding a pen is painful, use a larger or built-up pen. Nylon-tip or rolling-ball pens require less pressure than pencils and ball point pens.
- Install lever-type door handles instead of knobs on doors in your home.
- Use a utility cart to transport heavy items and to avoid extra trips when moving lawn supplies, unloading groceries and performing other tasks around the house.
- When traveling with luggage, use a lightweight cart with wheels, or buy luggage with built-in wheels.
- During any activity, sit instead of stand whenever possible.

It's a common mistake to choose a cane that's too long. This pushes one side of your body up, putting strain on your shoulder joint and arm muscles. And a cane that's too short causes you to lean forward, putting extra pressure on nerves in your wrist. Whether too long or too short, a cane that's not fitted properly may throw you off balance and make you less stable on your feet.

When buying a cane, don't base your decision on looks alone. A distinctive cane may add flair to your appearance, but there are more important factors to consider:

Select the right style. If you plan to use your cane daily, the traditional candy-cane style — with curved handle — probably isn't the best choice, especially if you have arthritis in your hands. This cane doesn't center your weight over the staff, which puts pressure on your hand. Instead, consider a swan-neck cane or one with a grip that straddles the pole part of the cane. In addition, a lightweight cane is less of a burden than a heavy one. If you have severe arthritis in your hand, a platform attachment that distributes the pressure over your entire forearm may be more comfortable.

Consider length. To determine the proper length, stand erect with your shoes on. Hold your arms at your sides. The length of the cane should equal the distance from the crease in your wrist to the floor.

When you hold your cane while standing still, your elbow should flex 15 to 20 degrees. Remember, if you plan to use the cane alternately with shoe heels of varying heights, make sure you get an adjustable cane. Nonadjustable canes can be cut to fit, but then the shoes you wear must all have the same heel height.

Get a good grip. A handle with a large diameter is generally easier to hold for extended periods. Make sure your fingers and thumb don't overlap when you grip the handle. If you have arthritis in your hands, ask your doctor or physical therapist to advise you about grip size.

Check the tip. Your cane should have a removable rubber tip, 1 to 2 inches wide, for good traction and safety. Check the tip regularly. Replace it before it wears down and becomes smooth.

For cold climates, you can get an attachable steel spike for times when you find yourself on a patch of ice.

You'll get the most from your cane if you hold it on the side opposite your weaker or painful hip, knee or leg, and move your weaker leg and the cane at the same time. This improves your balance and stability and takes stress off the painful or weaker side.

Put as much weight on your cane as necessary to make walking comfortable, stable and smooth.

When you go up stairs, lead with the cane and your "good" foot. Then follow with the "bad" foot. When you go down stairs, do the opposite. Either way, use the railing with your free hand.

Once you've obtained a cane that fits correctly and you've used it for a while, decide

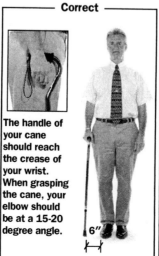

Correct

The handle of your cane should reach the crease of your wrist. When grasping the cane, your elbow should be at a 15-20 degree angle.

6"

Incorrect

Too short   Too long

if it's a help or hindrance. If you have a permanent disability, your cane may become your friendly, long-term companion. If you've recovered from joint replacement surgery for severe osteoarthritis, retire your cane.

Helpful hint: If you're receiving Medicare and your doctor writes a prescription for a cane, Medicare will share the cost. Most health insurance companies also provide coverage. But be sure to ask your physician to write "needed for walking" on the prescription.

Equipment resources

If you live in a city, the Yellow Pages of your telephone book will include the phone numbers of medical equipment suppliers in your area. You can reach many distant companies by calling a toll-free telephone number. Larger stores may ship you their catalog at no cost.

If you have a computer and Internet access, you can shop online. For information and some cautions on surfing the Web for health information and supplies, see Chapter 13.

Here are names and addresses of a sampling of medical equipment suppliers:

The Mayo Clinic Store
Siebens Building, Subway Level
Rochester, MN 55905
507-284-9669 or 888-303-9354
www.healthe-store.com
(order free catalog online)

AliMed
297 High Street
Dedham, MA 02026
800-225-2610
www.alimed.com

Anderson Wheelchair and
Therapeutic Supply
1117 Second St. S.W.
Rochester, MN 55902
507-288-0113

Sammons Preston
AbilityOne Corporation
4 Sammons Court
Bolingbrook, IL 60440
800-323-5547
www.sammonspreston.com

Aids for Arthritis
35 Wakefield Drive
Medford, NJ 08055
800-654-0707
www.aidsforarthritis.com

Sears Home Health and
Wellness Catalog
7700 Brush Hill Road.
Suite 240
Hinsdale, IL 60521
800-326-1750

Chapter 3

Exercising properly

K eep moving. That's good advice for almost everyone, whether arthritis is part of the picture or not. Remember this as you consider what kinds and amounts of exercise to do. This chapter discusses the benefits of exercise and helps you assess your fitness level and set goals. It also provides you with information and specific exercises to get started. However, it's important to acknowledge upfront that you're the expert. You alone know how you feel. Only you — with the benefit of experience — will know how much is too much. Your exercise program will become increasingly effective as you listen to your body and act accordingly.

Importance of exercise

For most of us, activity is essential to health. Aerobic exercise contributes greatly to cardiovascular fitness. Cardiovascular health is more than how hard your heart pumps and how well you breathe. It's complex. It involves how well your muscles and tissues take oxygen from your blood. It includes the density of the small blood vessels (capillaries) that feed your tissues. Body composition also affects cardiovascular health. So does your body's ability to handle fat or fat-like substances (lipids) found in your blood. Prolonged bed rest or inactivity aggravates these functions and leads to poor cardiovascular health. Inactivity causes reduced circulation in your legs. It also decreases your body's ability to use oxygen in your blood. Lack of exercise makes your bones less dense and causes your muscles to become weakened and lose flexibility. It may also contribute to feelings of dependency, discouragement and depression.

Exercise is part of the solution for the most frequent complaints of people with arthritis. Most people with arthritis say their No. 1 problem is pain. Appropriate types and amounts of exercise help reduce the pain that arthritis causes. The second most common complaint of people with arthritis is fatigue. The prescription for addressing fatigue is adequate rest and aerobic conditioning.

Years ago doctors recommended rest, joint protection and medication for people with arthritis — still an important part of good advice during flares. But a healthy balance between suitable exercise and rest is important. "Let comfort be your guide" is a good rule to follow. But be careful about skipping your exercise. It takes at least 3 days to come back from the fitness you lose during each day of inactivity. If a flare is preventing you from taking your usual 45-minute walk, don't drop your flexibility exercises. Try to accumulate the 45 minutes in smaller segments. If it's painful to walk on a hard surface, try riding a bicycle or walking in a swimming pool.

A sensible exercise program can reduce your risk of cardiovascular disease and increase your endurance. It can help slow bone loss that leads to a thinning of your bones, which makes them prone to breaking (osteoporosis). Appropriate exercise increases flexibility and strengthens the muscles that help stabilize your joints. It helps reduce morning stiffness and maintain mobility. It improves your balance and increases your endurance. And, especially important for people with arthritis, exercise can help you control your weight. This helps you avoid placing unnecessary stress on your joints. Exercise makes it easier to carry grocery bags, step in and out of the bathtub, get in and out of your car and avoid falls. In addition to these physical benefits, exercise boosts you psychologically and gives you a renewed sense of well-being. It's a fact that people with arthritis who are fit fare better than those who aren't.

Tailoring your program

A "one-size-fits-all" approach doesn't work for people with arthritis. The only expert on the subject of you is you. Learn to pay attention to your body. Your nervous system is a good source of information — if you're tuned in. Experience is the best teacher of what level of activity is appropriate for you. Remember how you feel as you begin an activity. When you're finished, note again how you feel. Are you the same or better? How about 2 hours — or 2 days — later? An activity level that's appropriate for you should make you feel the same or better afterward. If you feel worse, especially after several hours or the next day, there's something wrong with what you're doing. You may be overdoing it. Or you may be performing an activity in a way that aggravates your condition. When your body talks — listen. Don't repeat the same activity in the same way and at the same level the next day. Build up gradually or ask a physical therapist or your doctor to help you determine whether you're doing the activity most effectively.

Before you begin or change your exercise routine, have a thorough physical examination and discuss your plans with your doctor. It helps a lot if your doctor knows about your specific needs. Talk about whether you should consult with a physical therapist or an occupational therapist. These individuals are trained to help people find ways to move effectively. A therapist who has been successful working with people who have arthritis may often be very helpful. But here again, remember that you are the expert on the topic of you. A therapist — or even a doctor — can't know how you feel as well as you can.

A program that's well designed for you should include activities you enjoy. Some people enjoy exercising with family members or friends. Walking is a good way to start. Again, your goals can be very different from those of someone else with arthritis. And, as you listen to your body, your goals can change from day to day as your condition changes.

Some people with arthritis are glad when they can walk a step or two. Perhaps you can easily walk several miles. In either case walking is an excellent activity for overall conditioning. It improves cardiovascular health and bone density. Walking also helps your muscles and joints get nourishment. It leads to improved flexibility, strength and balance, which can help prevent stumbles from becoming falls. If you don't enjoy walking, you may prefer swimming, water aerobics or cross-country skiing or biking, either outdoors or on stationary machines indoors. These fitness activities help you manage your normal daily activities without becoming winded or dizzy, breaking into a sweat or experiencing fatigue. They also help you control your weight, sleep better and improve your sense of well-being.

Include activities several times each day to improve flexibility. Stretching and range-of-motion exercises counteract the stiffness that arthritis causes in your major joints and spine. Muscles that have a high level of elasticity are less susceptible to injury. Again, a doctor or physical therapist can tell you the proper way to stretch a muscle, but only you know when it's stretched too far or for too long. Moderate, regular exercise is the emphasis of guidelines from the Centers for Disease Control and Prevention, the American Heart Association, the American College of Sports Medicine and others. The frequency and duration of activity are more important than the intensity.

Your activity goals

Guidelines recommend at least 30 minutes of low to moderately intense physical activity most days. Be creative about including exercise in your lifestyle. Watch TV news while you're on a treadmill. Read a magazine or book while you ride a stationary bicycle. Schedule exercise into your day as you would a round of golf. Although sustained, continuous exercise may give the greatest benefit, you don't need to do all of your exercise at one time during the day. You also benefit from short periods of activity, perhaps in 5- to 10-minute intervals, that add up to at least 30 minutes. The key is the total amount of energy expended, not the intensity. If you can't carry on a conversation or if you experience severe pain while you exercise, you're probably pushing too hard. Walking with family or friends can be a way to combine exercise with quality time together. Walking with children provides them with a role model for lifetime habits of healthy activity.

High-impact activities, such as jogging, basketball and some aerobics classes, put stress on your joints and may aggravate your symptoms. Substitute low-intensity activities, such as walking for pleasure, low-impact social dancing or gentle water exercise. If you are able, use moderately intense activities, such as brisk walking, swimming, water aerobics, bicycling, cross-country skiing, low-impact aerobic dancing or rowing.

Organized programs

Some people enjoy participating in one or more of the numerous exercise programs that address special needs of people with arthritis. Your doctor or physical therapist can provide information about whether these routines may suit your needs. Many routines focus on simple chair

Every move counts

Normal daily activities, as well as formal exercise sessions, add up. You get health benefits from carrying out the trash, cleaning, shopping, vacuuming, making the bed and mowing the lawn. But consider these activities a supplement to, not a substitute for, your regular exercises. And don't forget to balance these tasks with rest.

You can boost your exercise total by increasing physical activity in your routine daily tasks. Park your car farther away from your destination and walk a little farther. Or walk your dog farther than around the block.

A word of warning: Remember that body mechanics and positioning during exercise are very important. Poor positioning or body mechanics can make joints more painful or cause swelling. Some positions may be stressful to certain joints. For example, if you can't find a comfortable position for vacuuming, ask a physical therapist to help you find a comfortable position.

exercises and arm and leg movements, using light weights and frequent repetitions for upper and lower body conditioning. Be careful with frequent repetition, especially if you have rheumatoid arthritis, because it can aggravate joint pain. Chair exercises don't help maintain bone strength as well as weight-bearing exercises do. If you're able, add walking to such a routine. When gauging an exercise program, take into consideration your other daily activities. Make sure you don't exercise a joint or muscle group too much. Programs you may wish to consider include those listed here.

Water exercise. Water exercises are especially beneficial. Soothing, warm water (between 83 F and 90 F) relaxes your muscles. Your buoyancy in water relieves stress on joints, and the water offers muscle-strengthening resistance. Every year, thousands of people participate in the Arthritis Foundation's aquatic exercise programs. For more information, call your local Arthritis Foundation chapter (listed in your phone book's white pages) or the national office at 800-283-7800.

Tai chi (TIE-chee). People use the ancient Chinese martial art of tai chi to relax and strengthen muscles and joints and reduce tension in the body and mind. Tai chi's slow, deliberate circular movements and postures combined with deep, regular breathing can increase circulation, relax the mind and body and ease chronic pain. As you concentrate on your body's motions, you feel both alert and tranquil, an effect that has earned tai chi the label "moving meditation." Your local health club or YMCA may offer tai chi classes.

Videos. Numerous exercise videos are designed specifically for people with arthritis. Some videos may contain movements not appropriate for your level of strength or ability. Discuss each exercise on the video with your physical therapist. Discontinue movements that seem too difficult, cause pain or cause joint swelling.

- The Arthritis Foundation has developed a set of two videos, *People With Arthritis Can Exercise (PACE)*. Level 1 offers gentle routines that include stretching, strengthening and fitness exercises, and Level 2 is a moderate program designed to increase range of motion and endurance.
- *Pool Exercise Program (PEP)* is a video designed to help you increase and maintain joint flexibility, strengthen and tone muscles and increase endurance. Exercises are performed in water at chest level. Call your local library, arthritis support group or Arthritis Foundation chapter to borrow these tapes. To purchase them, log on to *www.arthritis.org/AFstore* or call the national membership center office at 800-207-8633.

Chances are, you'll stick with your exercise program if it's fun. But give it enough time. People who maintain a new behavior for 6 months usually have long-term success as it becomes a habit. Many health clubs offer classes for exercise novices. Make your goal exercise — a reward itself — rather than a "slow" goal such as losing weight.

Assess your fitness

Fitness has numerous components, including aerobic capacity, muscular fitness, appropriate body composition and good posture. Earlier in this chapter, the discussion on cardiovascular fitness described the benefits of aerobic exercise — exercise with oxygen. Aerobic exercise causes your body to use extra oxygen and calories continuously. Walking, biking, swimming and cross-country skiing are good aerobic exercises for people with arthritis.

Muscular fitness is a general term. It includes flexibility, range of motion, endurance and strength. Range of motion refers to how far and in what direction a joint will move. It also measures a muscle's capacity to stretch. If your muscles can't stretch far enough, your joint may be fine,

Tai chi for chronic pain

Tai chi was developed more than 1,000 years ago. Literally hundreds of combinations of movement are involved in tai chi. But the focus of the exercise remains consistent: combining concentration, stretching, balance and grace. Doing tai chi daily can increase range of motion and strengthen muscles for an in-depth mind and body workout.

Although there are several schools of thought for learning tai chi, all focus on these essentials:

- *Your body is relaxed.* Motion is even and fluid. Your body is balanced and steady. Muscles aren't rigid, and breathing is deep and steady.
- *Your mind is tranquil but alert.* You concentrate on movement.
- *Your body movements are coordinated.* Hands, eyes, trunk and limbs perform as a whole. Movements are gentle, and you're constantly moving.

These exercises are just part of one group of tai chi movements. You do all movements in the group as one fluid motion.

but its range of motion will be limited. Stretches are good for improving flexibility. However, they may be challenging and painful if you have severe osteoarthritis or rheumatoid arthritis. It's easy to hurt yourself by stretching too much. Remember, you have the best information about yourself — direct from your nervous system. Avoid stretching a muscle to the point of pain.

If you have arthritis, activities designed for specific strengthening often are very challenging. Before adding strengthening exercises to your program, consult a physical therapist experienced in working with people who have arthritis. You should receive careful instruction. Review your progress with the therapist periodically. You're less likely to hurt yourself and more likely to enjoy exercise if you begin an exercise program with walking and range-of-motion activities.

Body composition refers to the proportions of bone, muscle and fat in your body. Are you lean and muscular or overweight? Inappropriate body composition contributes to the pain of arthritis. Osteoarthritis also worsens if you're overweight. Having excess pounds to carry around increases your fatigue. If you're realistic, you can probably judge your body composition by looking at yourself in the mirror. For help determining whether you're truly overweight, talk to your doctor. If you are overweight, reasonable weight loss will increase your energy and endurance.

Good posture is important for everyone. But it's especially important when you have arthritis. Many people with arthritis have increased pain as a result of poor posture. If you're not aerobically fit, your body may tend to sag. Lack of endurance can reduce your ability to hold your body in good posture. The solution to posture problems isn't as simple as your mother's direction to "straighten up."

Good posture doesn't mean holding yourself in a rigid or sway-backed position. Normally, a person with good posture shifts constantly. Movement brings nutrition to your cartilage and joint surfaces. In fact, the wiggling movements of a 5-year-old are very conducive to good posture, but sitting all day is not. The easiest way to improve your posture is through walking. The faster you walk, the harder your muscles must work to keep you upright and straight and from falling over. Some people find that swimming also helps improve their posture.

The following self-assessment tests help you judge your current fitness level. If the activities described are too strenuous, ask your doctor or physical therapist for an appropriate substitute. Before you do any of these activities, warm up the muscles used for that activity by stretching them gently or do range-of-motion exercises. Start an exercise journal. Make notes to use as benchmarks in tracking your progress.

Aerobic fitness

Take a walking test for a distance you can manage, whether it's 10 feet or a mile. Find a place where you can walk on a level surface — in your living room, or perhaps in a park or on a school track. Note the time on your watch and begin walking at a comfortable pace. Walk as briskly as you comfortably can. If you're too winded to carry on a conversation, you're walking too fast. After you walk the distance you've determined, check your watch and record your time.

Muscular fitness

- To check your upper body strength, do push-ups. Do this cautiously, or substitute another activity if your arthritis affects your hands, wrists, elbows or shoulders. Stand an arm's length from a wall with your palms flat on the wall. Lean into the wall, then push away. Repeat. Stop when you need to rest and record how many push-ups you did.
- To check your balance, stand near a wall (in case you begin to fall). Record how long you can stand on each foot alone.
- To measure your hamstring flexibility and strength, sit in a chair. Straighten your knees as far as you can in front of you. Measure the distance of your heel from the floor or notice the angle of your knee. Be careful not to hurt your back.
- With one hand at a time, reach behind you and as far as you can across your back.

Posture

- Observe and note your body posture as you stand facing a full-length mirror. Your ear should be in line with your instep. Your lower spine will curve in slightly.
- Stand upright with your heels next to the wall, resting your buttocks, back and head on the wall. You should have a space to fit your arm between your lower back and the wall.
- Sit in a chair with your buttocks at the back of the chair and your feet resting flat on the floor. Your thighs should be parallel to the floor.

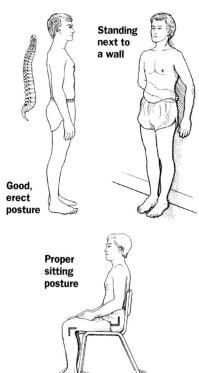

Standing next to a wall

Good, erect posture

Proper sitting posture

Getting started

Exercise whenever it's best for you. Loosen up with exercises first thing in the morning. Or wait until later, when you're less stiff — or even toward the end of the day. Exercising later — 4 to 5 hours before bedtime — may help you sleep better and feel less stiff in the morning. Don't exercise right after you eat. Move with a slow, steady rhythm. Don't jerk or bounce. Don't hold your breath, because this deprives your muscles of oxygen and tires them. Maintain good posture while you exercise.

Avoid exercising tender, injured or severely inflamed joints. If you feel new joint pain, stop. New pain that lasts more than 2 hours after you exercise probably means you've overdone it. Rest and take an over-the-counter pain reliever as needed. Next time, break the activity into smaller segments or reduce the intensity or number of repetitions. If pain persists for more than a few days, call your doctor. With some creativity, you can continue gentle exercises during a flare, unless you have a fractured bone. If a flare in your knee limits your walking distance, try a cane, walk in a swimming pool or use a stationary bicycle set with no resistance.

Warm up your muscles with a warm shower, heat packs or massage before exercising. But don't apply heat to an already inflamed joint. After exercise it may help to apply either heat or cold to affected joints for 10 to 15 minutes. If you're not regularly taking an anti-inflammatory medication and if heat and cold don't relieve your pain, aspirin, another nonsteroidal anti-inflammatory drug or acetaminophen taken 1 hour before exercise may limit swelling and reduce pain. Avoid mixing medications. Don't overmedicate because you're then masking the pain that warns you to stop. If you already treat your pain with daily medication and can't exercise without pain, you may need the help of a physical therapist. Don't force an exercise or motion. Start gradually. You may feel slight discomfort but should not feel new pain. Try doing less more frequently throughout the day.

Always allow time to warm up with gentle range-of-motion exercises. Gently stretch your hamstring muscles (see page 48) or begin walking slowly. Start flexibility exercises (see pages 40 to 46). At first you may tire rapidly. Try to walk or do range-of-motion exercises each day for 5 minutes. As you comfortably can, add exercise or increase your pace. Add time gradually, until you exercise a minimum of 30 minutes at least four times each week. Keep your goals manageable. Perhaps you can only walk a minute each day at first. But if you add a minute each week, you'll be walking nearly an hour each day after a year. Slow down and let your muscles and heart rate return to normal during the final 5 to 10 minutes of each session.

Warning signs

It's important to listen to your body carefully when you have arthritis. You'll learn by trial and error how much is too much. Pay attention to how you feel before and after you exercise. Rule No. 1: If you feel the same or better, it's working. If you feel worse, it's not.

Introduce new activities gradually and heed warning signs. Call your doctor immediately if you experience chest pain, severe shortness of breath, faintness, dizziness or nausea. If exercise brings on a cramp or muscle pain, gently rub and stretch the muscle until the pain subsides. If the pain persists and your limb loses its color, see a doctor immediately.

Finish your session with slow, easy movements. If you experience new pain later in the day or fatigue the following day, you've probably done too much too fast or an inappropriate activity. You may need a new activity. Your doctor or physical therapist can advise you.

Gather your equipment

The most important equipment is a comfortable, supportive pair of athletic shoes appropriate for the exercise you do. Always replace shoes before wear causes foot pain. You can buy special handles for sports equipment — golf clubs and table tennis paddles, for example — and garden tools. An occupational therapist can advise you.

Be cautious about adding weights. Weights can aggravate joint pain and increase swelling, especially when your arthritis is very active. Don't spend a lot of money on weight-training equipment. Fill old socks with beans or pennies or use canned food. Some athletic equipment stores sell weights by the pound. Or check your newspaper's classified ads for used sets. Doctors and therapists frequently recommend that people with rheumatoid arthritis use light weights or exercise without weights.

Recommended exercises

If you can walk, walking is your best bet for a starter exercise. If you can't walk, try a stationary bicycle with no resistance or do hand or arm exercises. It's good to move each joint in its full range of motion every day. The following descriptions may jog your memory of what you've learned in physical therapy. If you don't understand them, talk with your therapist or doctor or look for them on a recommended video.

Flexibility exercises

These exercises help maintain normal joint function and relieve stiffness. Do an assortment of them for 5 to 10 minutes several times each day. As you can, gradually add a few repetitions. Avoid pain.

Your neck:

- Bring your head forward, as though to touch your chin to your chest. Return your head upright. Use care with rheumatoid arthritis.
- Tilt your ear to your left shoulder without raising your shoulders. Return your head upright. Repeat to the right.
- Turn your face to the left, keeping neck, shoulders and trunk straight. Repeat to the right.

Your shoulders:

- With your arms at your side, roll your shoulders forward in a circular motion. Reverse.
- Stand with your feet shoulder-width apart. Hold a cane, broomstick or wand comfortably with both hands (1). Raise the cane forward and upward over your head (2). Return to the starting position. Repeat. You may place your palms up (as in illustration) or down.

1

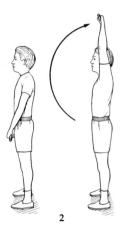

2

• To exercise one arm, hold the cane vertically in front of you. Place the arm to be exercised higher on the cane (3). Your lower arm may push to help raise your upper arm.

3

• Stand with your feet shoulder-width apart. Grasp the cane with both hands, palm up on the hand you are exercising (4). Raise your arm out to the side (not in front of you). Continue, until your arm touches your ear. Return to the starting position. Change hands and repeat (5).

4   5

• Stand with your feet shoulder-width
apart. Hold the cane behind your back,
with your hands shoulder-width apart
(6). Slowly move the cane backward
and upward, keeping your elbows
straight (7). All movement should
come from your shoulders. Don't lean
forward to get more motion. Return to
the starting position. Repeat.

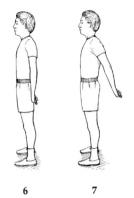

6   7

8   9   10

• With arms out to your sides, bend your elbows and hold the cane in
front of your chest (8). Gently move the cane in an upward arc toward
your head (9). Try not to move your upper arms. Repeat. Move the
cane over your head and lower it to the base of your neck (10). Repeat.

  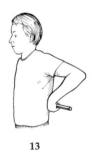

11   12   13

• With your arms out to your sides, bend your elbows and hold the
cane in front of your chest (11). Gently move the cane in a downward
arc toward your stomach (12). If you can, position the cane behind
your hips, with your palms facing behind you. Slowly raise the cane
up along your back toward your shoulder blades (13). Repeat.

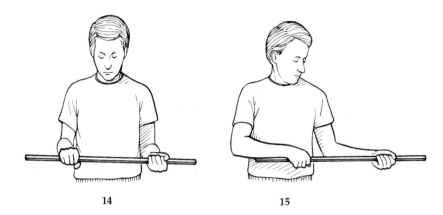

14   15

- With your upper arms against your body, bend your elbows and grasp the cane with palm up on the arm that will move outward (14). The palm on the arm that will move inward faces down. Gently slide the cane across your body so that one forearm swings outward from your body while the other one swings inward toward your stomach (15). Repeat. Change palm positions and repeat.
- Place your right palm behind your neck and the back of your left hand in the small of your back. Gently attempt to touch your hands behind your back. Reverse.
- Clasp your hands behind your head. Slowly breathe in as you gently move your elbows back and release your breath as you relax your elbows forward.
- Bring both elbows to shoulder height. Ease your elbows backward and feel a slight (not painful) stretch in your chest muscles.

Your elbows:

- Bend both elbows, bringing your forearm up until your fingers touch your shoulders. Straighten arms.
- Keep your upper arms next to your body while bending your elbows to form a right angle. Turn your palms toward the ceiling, then toward the floor.

Your wrists:

- Keep your upper arms at your side and bend your elbows to form a right angle. Hold your hands out with your thumbs facing upward. Move both hands toward your stomach, then facing out as far as possible.

Your hands and fingers:

- Bend your thumb across your palm to touch the base of your little finger.
- Bend and straighten the end and middle joints of your fingers (16). Keep your knuckles straight. Relax and repeat with each hand.
- Bend your fingers to make a fist. Bend each joint as much as possible (17). Relax and repeat with each hand.

16   17

- Straighten your fingers (18). Relax and repeat with each hand. Make an "O" by touching your thumb to each fingertip (19). Open your hand wide (20). Relax and repeat.

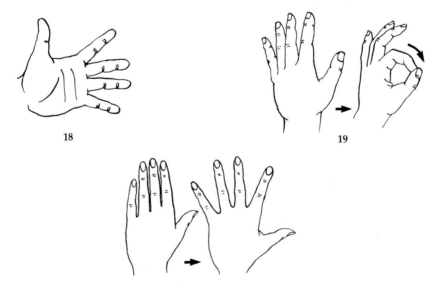

18   19

20

Your hips:

- While standing, lift your knee toward your chest to make a right angle. Alternate legs to march in place. Try this while lying on your back, too. Keep one leg extended as the other leg is bent. Grasp the back of the thigh of your bent leg and gently pull it toward your chest. Don't force your leg. Repeat with the other leg.
- Stand and face a chair. Hold onto the back of the chair for support. Gently move one straight leg out to the side and return. Repeat with the other leg. You can also do this exercise lying down, sliding one leg at a time out to the side and back to midline.
- Lie on your back, feet together, toes pointed up. Slide one leg to the side. Keep your toes pointed to the ceiling. Turn your foot in, then out. Return your leg to midline. Repeat with the other leg.

Your knees:

- Hold onto the back of a chair as you stand on one foot. Keep your knees together. Gently flex your knee and bring one foot up. Alternate. Don't arch your back. You can do this lying on your stomach, with a pillow supporting your stomach and hips. Keep one leg extended. Bring the other foot up toward the back of your thigh by bending your knee. Don't force your knee to an uncomfortable angle. Return your leg to an extended position. Repeat with the other leg.
- Lie on your back. Bend your knee to place one foot flat. Slide the heel as close to your buttock as possible, then extend. Repeat with the other leg.

- Sit in a chair with your ankles crossed. Push your feet against each other. Put the other foot in front and repeat.

Your calves:

- Stand an arm's length from the wall, with one foot forward. Place your hands on the wall at shoulder level (21). Keep your back straight as you lean toward the wall with your hips (but not to the point of pain). Relax and repeat with the other leg.

Your hamstrings:

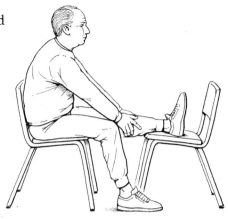

22

- Sit in a chair with one leg on another chair (22). Keep your back straight. Slowly bend forward at your hip until you feel a slight stretch in the back of your thigh. Repeat with the other leg.

Your ankles and feet (skip these exercises if they are painful):

- Stand with your feet about 12 inches apart. Rise to your toes with both feet. Relax to the starting position. Rise to the toes of your right foot. Relax. Rise to the toes of both feet. Relax. Rise to the toes of your left foot. Relax. Repeat.
- Walk on your heels.
- Walk on your toes.
- Walk heel to toe, as if on a tightrope.
- While standing, lift your left foot and place it to the right of your right foot. Repeat with left foot planted, placing your right foot to the left of your left foot. This is called braiding.

Remember: Seek medical advice before you begin any exercise program. Your physician or physical therapist can instruct you in exercises specially suited to your needs.

Strengthening exercises

After warming up with flexibility exercises, do these several times a week — only if you can do so without adding new pain. Don't use weights at first. As you gain strength, you may gradually add weight and repetitions. Isometric exercises, which involve no movement, can be very beneficial for people with arthritis.

Your daily back routine

Walking is the most important way to exercise the muscles of your back. In addition to walking, a wide variety of exercises to stretch and strengthen your back and supporting muscles are available. A few of the most commonly prescribed maneuvers are shown here.

Cat stretch. **Step 1: Get down on your hands and knees. Slowly let your back and abdomen sag toward the floor. Step 2: Slowly arch your back away from the floor. Repeat several times.**

Half sit-up. **Lie on your back on a firm surface with your knees bent and feet flat. With your arms outstretched, reach toward your knees with your hands until your shoulder blades no longer touch the ground. Don't grasp your knees. Hold for a few seconds and slowly return to the starting position. Repeat several times.**

Shoulder-blade squeeze. **Sit upright on a chair. Keep your chin tucked in and your shoulders down. Pull your shoulder blades together and straighten your upper back. Hold a few seconds. Return to starting position. Repeat several times.**

Leg lift. **Lie face down on a firm surface with a large pillow under your hips and lower abdomen. Keeping your knee bent, raise one leg slightly off the surface and hold for about 5 seconds. Repeat several times.**

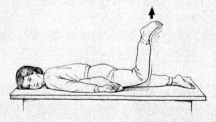

• Chair sit-ups — Skip this exercise if your
hands, wrists and elbows are painful. Sit
in a sturdy chair that has arms (no
wheels), with your feet firmly on the floor.
Push your body up off the surface of the
chair using your arms only (23). Relax
and repeat.

23

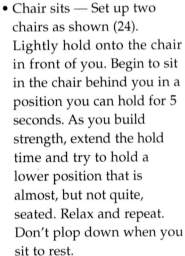

24

• Chair sits — Set up two
chairs as shown (24).
Lightly hold onto the chair
in front of you. Begin to sit
in the chair behind you in a
position you can hold for 5
seconds. As you build
strength, extend the hold
time and try to hold a
lower position that is
almost, but not quite,
seated. Relax and repeat.
Don't plop down when you
sit to rest.

• Quadriceps — Sit or lie down on your back with one leg extended,
foot supported and knee straight. Push your knee straight by tightening the muscles on the front of your thigh. Imagine that your leg
is getting longer. Repeat with your other leg.

• Hamstring — Sit or lie down on your back with your knee slightly
bent. Push down on your flat heel by tightening the muscles at the
back of your thigh. Repeat with your other leg.

• Gluteus — Lie face down, legs extended. Squeeze your buttocks
together. Relax.

• Lie on your back, legs flat on the bed. Weave a belt snugly in a figure eight around both legs just above your knees (25). Pull with both legs equally to spread them apart as far as the belt allows, keeping toes, legs and knees extended straight. Relax.

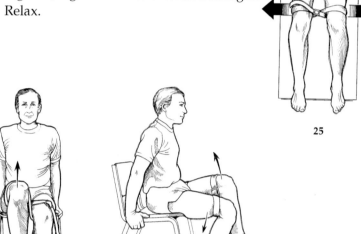

25

26

• Sit on the edge of a chair. Weave a belt snugly in a figure eight around both legs just above your knees (26). Pulling your legs in opposite directions, lift one leg up off the chair. Relax. Repeat with the other leg.

• Sit on the edge of a chair. Weave a belt snugly in a figure eight around both ankles (27). Attempt to straighten one knee while pulling the other foot backward, applying equal force with both legs. Relax. Repeat with the other leg.

27

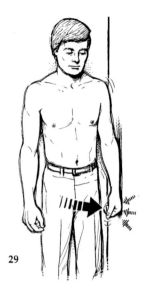

28   29   30

- Stand facing a wall, arms at your side. Keeping a straight elbow, move one arm forward and press the back of your hand against the wall (28). Repeat with the other hand.
- Stand sideways next to a wall, arms at your side (29). Push the back of the hand near the wall out to the side against the wall. Turn and repeat with your other hand.
- Stand with your back against a wall, arms hanging straight at your side (30). Keeping your elbow straight, push first one then the other arm back against the wall.

Aerobic fitness (endurance)

Begin an aerobic exercise program gradually, slowly increasing the amount and time. Try to build up to at least 30 minutes of aerobic activity 4 or more days a week, adding a minute or two over a period of days or weeks. If you're comfortable with your pace and want an additional challenge, gradually increase to 45 to 60 minutes, 5 days a week. This program promotes aerobic conditioning and appropriate body composition and helps prevent osteoporosis.

Use your journal to recheck your fitness level occasionally. Listen to your body. Use the resources available to you. A good exercise program will not only renew your energy but also provide new fun and friends.

Chapter 4

Tips on pain control

Sharp. Throbbing. Nagging. Stiff. Burning. Achy. Agonizing. There may be 40 million different descriptions of arthritis pain, one for each person who has arthritis. If you're like most people with arthritis, you know that no matter how you describe it, that pain could keep you from the things you would like to do today. It just won't go away. You have to deal with your pain.

Your pain is influenced by several things: your level of activity, your physical condition, the amount of swelling in your joints, your tolerance for pain and your state of mind.

Your approach to treatment may be just as individual as your pain. Some approaches focus on building a lifestyle that minimizes pain. You can protect your painful joints by limiting movement and using devices to help with daily tasks (see Chapter 2). You can strengthen the muscles around your joint to keep it from taking the brunt of painful movements (see Chapter 3). Losing weight also may lessen the stress on painful joints (see Chapter 5). Maintaining an attitude that keeps pain in perspective is essential (see Chapter 6). The use of medication to reduce inflammation and treat pain is discussed in Chapter 7.

In many ways, this entire book is about the single most important symptom of arthritis: pain. And there are many ways to view and deal with it.

This chapter focuses on specific techniques for managing pain. The first section explains simple treatments for acute pain. Many of these can be performed at home. The second section discusses professional treatments other than medications.

Treating pain at home

Cold

For occasional flare-ups, cold may dull the sensation of pain in the first day or two. Cold has a numbing effect and decreases muscle spasms. Don't use cold treatments if you have poor circulation or numbness.

Ice packs. Before using an ice pack, apply a thin layer of mineral oil to your skin at the painful joint. Place a damp towel over the mineral oil. Finally, put the ice pack on the damp towel and cover it with several dry towels for insulation.

You may apply cold several times a day, but for no more than 15 or 20 minutes at a time. Check your skin regularly for loss of its underlying normal color. This color loss may indicate the onset of frostbite. Stop immediately if this happens.

Helpful hint: To make your own ice pack, combine ⅓ cup of rubbing alcohol with ⅔ cup of water. Place this mixture inside a freezer bag and seal it, then place the first bag inside a second, seal that and place in the freezer. The pack is ready to use when the contents are slushy. To re-freeze the contents after use, place in the freezer.

Ice massage. This method applies cold directly to your skin. Using a circular motion, move the ice in and around your painful joint for 5 to 7 minutes. Apply mild pressure and remember to keep the ice moving when it's in contact with your skin.

Again, remember to watch for color changes in your skin. If you notice your skin losing its underlying natural tone, stop immediately. If your skin becomes numb during the massage, end the treatment early.

Helpful hint: You can make your own ice block by freezing water in a paper cup. Peel back part of the cup to expose enough ice for your massage. Wrap the cup in a small towel to protect your hands.

Heat

Heat can ease your pain, relax tense, painful muscles and increase blood flow to the affected region. But if you have poor circulation or numbness in the part you plan to treat, don't apply heat. You won't know if you are getting burned. Don't apply heat after acute trauma or over a swollen area because it could increase swelling and pain.

Hot packs and heating pads. Apply several layers of towels over the area to be heated with a hot pack. Lay the hot pack over the towels. Cover the hot pack with several layers of towels for insulation. Add or remove towels between your skin and the hot pack to vary the heat. You may need to add layers of towels over spots where bones project. Apply the heat for 20 to 30 minutes.

Check your skin every 15 minutes. If you see red and white blotches, stop the treatment at once. Your skin has been heated enough. Continued heating could cause a burn or blister.

To protect your skin from burning, don't lie on a hot pack or heating pad or apply pressure during treatment. If your skin has poor sensation or if you have poor circulation, don't use heat treatment.

Heat lamps. Use a radiant heat lamp with a 250-watt reflector heat bulb. This bulb produces the type of infrared rays that cause a significant increase in local circulation in the skin and underlying tissues. Position the lamp 18 to 20 inches from your skin. Apply the heat for 20 to 30 minutes. As with hot packs or heating pads, use an alarm clock or timer, or ask someone to wake you if you think you might fall asleep.

You can decrease the intensity of the heat by moving the lamp farther away. Direct the lamp at the skin from the side rather than from above.

Hot and cold packs

Perhaps the safest and most convenient commercially available product for applying either heat or cold to an affected area is the inexpensive, reusable gel-filled pack found in most pharmacies.

You can heat the pack in hot water or a microwave oven or freeze it for application as a cold pack. The heat or cold dissipates as the pack is used, so it's safe to leave on for 20 or 30 minutes at a time. You can also use it to treat minor muscle sprains and strains and minor tendinitis.

Water: baths, showers, whirlpools. One of the easiest and most effective ways to apply heat is to take a 15-minute hot shower or bath. You don't need an expensive hot tub. A standard bathtub can be just as effective. However, in any very warm bath or shower, use extra caution — and the grab bars. You could become lightheaded or even faint.

Contrast baths

Contrast baths are helpful to many people with rheumatoid arthritis or osteoarthritis of the hands and feet. These baths may provide more relief than hot or cold baths alone.

Start with two large pans. Fill one pan with warm water (110 F) and the other with cool water (65 F). Place your joint in the warm water first for 10 minutes and then in the cold water for 1 minute. Cycle back to the warm water for 4 minutes and then to the cold for 1 minute and repeat this process for half an hour. Always end with the warm water. If pans aren't handy, twin sinks work just as well.

Helpful hint: Use warm, not hot, water.

Professional help for pain

Several health care workers may be part of your pain management team: your family physician, rheumatologist, physical therapist and occupational therapist, a physiatrist, psychiatrist or psychologist and perhaps even a practitioner of complementary medicine such as acupuncture. They may use various methods and techniques to help you manage your pain.

Physical control of pain

Exercise. Exercise is perhaps your best defense against pain. A physical therapist may work with you to develop an exercise program that maximizes your range of motion and strengthens your muscles around painful joints. A complete discussion of the benefits of exercise is found in Chapter 3.

Massage. Massage can improve your circulation, help you relax, decrease local pain and reduce swelling. Some therapists are specially trained in massage techniques for people with arthritis.

If you would like to give yourself a massage or train a family member to do it, remember to stop if the massage is painful. If your joint is very

The athlete

I was 26 years old when rheumatoid arthritis was diagnosed.

The news struck with shocking force. I had a husband and an infant son to care for. And I had been an athletic young woman, with high school championships in tennis and swimming. Living in Colorado, I also loved skiing throughout the long winter. In the warmer months my husband and I would bike with our friends up and over the spectacular mountain passes.

When the pain set in, it concentrated mainly in my feet and hands. Sharp pain. Dull pain. Throbbing pain. Every kind of pain you can imagine. Every step I took and every gripping action I made became horribly painful. The sensation of a single step, for instance, was akin to walking on a broken foot. The pain would begin in my joints and instantly engulf the entire foot.

My physician told me to stay as active as I possibly could. So when I was forced to give up some of my favorite pastimes, I tried to substitute others. I quit skiing but substituted snowshoeing. I gave up tennis, but became an enthusiastic hiker, walking as many as 5 miles at a stretch up and down towering mountainsides. Even with medication the pain was always there. But I learned to distract myself with thoughts: the beauty of the view, the chance to be outside in the fresh air, the sense of accomplishment I'd feel when the exercise was over.

Today, nearly all the pain is gone. The rheumatoid arthritis has been in remission for about a decade, and the osteoarthritis I got about the same time doesn't bother me. I get occasional pain in my hips, but prescribed exercises keep the joints strong and the pain at bay. My physician had said the pain might burn itself out, but I think my commitment to staying active helped a lot. I still swim a mile every day. And I've now biked in 49 states and 21 countries. In fact, even with my knee replacement 5 years ago, I just went on a 2-week bike trip across Portugal and celebrated my 70th birthday while I was there.

Cynthia
Denver, Colo.

swollen or painful, skip the massage of the joint and instead massage adjacent muscles. Also try a warming or cooling treatment to the joint or muscles or both. And, when giving a massage, use a lotion or massage oil to help your hands glide smoothly over the skin.

Helpful hint: If you use a massage oil or lotion, wash it off before any heat treatment to avoid burns.

Additional heat treatments. Unlike the more simplified home heat treatments, a physical therapist may use specialized techniques or equipment to provide pain relief.

Heat treatments might include soaking sore joints, particularly your hands, in a warm paraffin bath. For deep heat penetration, a physical therapist can use ultrasound or shortwave diathermy. This technique requires monitoring and can worsen some forms of arthritis. With instruction by a physical therapist, you may be able to use warm paraffin at home.

Steroid injections. Steroids reduce pain and inflammation. Your doctor may occasionally inject a cortisone drug into an acutely inflamed joint — for example, your hip, knee or ankle.

Because frequent steroid injections can accelerate joint damage, your doctor may limit the number of injections to no more than two or three each year.

Nerve block. This is an anesthetic injection that deadens the nerves to a painful area. Its use is limited because the pain relief may last only a short time.

TENS. Transcutaneous electronic nerve stimulation (TENS) stops pain by blocking nerve signals from reaching your brain. A therapist tapes electrodes on your skin at the site of your pain. The electrodes are linked to a battery-operated stimulator, which delivers a tiny, painless electrical current.

TENS may also help release hormones (endorphins) that fight pain. If TENS is helpful, your doctor may prescribe a unit for you to use at home. Many insurance companies and Medicare require that your doctor document the effectiveness of TENS before they'll provide coverage for a home unit. This requires that you take note of any improvement of function and reduction of pain.

Complementary and alternative treatments. Other treatments such as acupuncture are gaining acceptance in the medical community. A complete discussion can be found in Chapter 9.

Psychological control of pain

Maintaining a positive attitude is essential to coping with chronic pain (see Chapter 6). However, you may reach a point at which you need some extra support or training to cope successfully. This can be an opportunity to discover a new approach to taking charge of your arthritis.

Behavior therapy. The goal of behavior therapy is to identify and modify some of your reactions to the pain, as well as to make changes to better manage your life despite your pain. This approach may include making changes in your daily routine and incorporating a balance of activities to maintain your ability to be active. You may learn to cope more effectively with changes in your lifestyle, evaluate your priorities and your response to stress, and understand and accept your pain.

Related treatments. In addition to learning behavior approaches to managing your pain, there are related treatments that can improve your functioning and may lessen your pain.

Biofeedback. Your body has some automatic reactions to stress: muscle tension, changes in skin temperature and changes in blood pressure and heart rate. The goal of biofeedback is to teach you to recognize your body's reactions to pain and learn to modify them.

During a session with a therapist, you are attached to monitors that track your physiologic systems — heart, respiration, muscle tension and skin temperature. The therapist will help you learn to reduce the symptoms of stress throughout your body through relaxation techniques.

Relaxation training. You can learn several ways to relax your body and mind. These include progressive muscle relaxation, deep breathing, guided imagery and meditation exercises.

One of the most commonly used strategies for pain is progressive muscle relaxation. You learn to focus on each muscle progressively. First, you tense a muscle and hold the tension for 5 or 10 seconds, focusing on the sensations of tension and identifying specific muscles or muscle groups. Then, you slowly release the muscle while focusing on the sensations of relaxation and released tension. This procedure is repeated in the major muscle groups of your body so that you become familiar with the sensation of relaxing your entire body.

The ideal setting for learning relaxation is a quiet room where you can rest comfortably on the floor or in a reclining chair or bed. You need to feel relatively at ease but not tired. An instructor can be a great help in directing your attention. You will learn to concentrate and to relax at the same time — and be able to do it yourself at home. You may listen to a tape, although live training may be more effective. Eventually, you learn to relax without verbal cues from another person.

The goal of any relaxation strategy is to reduce the level of tension in your body. You can use relaxation throughout the day, when you feel tension or pain building. In this way you may prevent a worsening of the tension or pain and successfully complete your activities. For more information on deep breathing, guided imagery and meditation exercises, see Chapter 6.

Chronic pain centers. If your pain is severe, your doctor may recommend that you visit a chronic pain center. In this setting, you may participate for several days and work with physicians and therapists representing various specialties. Some centers require overnight stays, whereas others offer outpatient treatments.

This team approach is essential because it's unlikely that any one technique will work in controlling your pain. The professionals in an interdisciplinary center can treat both your pain and its potential consequences, such as disruption within a marriage and family, loss of income, depression and anxiety.

Chapter 5

Eating for better health

The food choices you make each day can have a significant effect on your overall health and sense of well-being. If you aren't eating a balanced diet, you may feel fatigued. Eating too much of the wrong kinds of foods also can cause you to gain weight, which can worsen your pain and lower your self-esteem. To feel healthy, you need to eat healthy. A balanced diet can give you added energy, improve how you feel and help you control your weight.

If you think of healthy eating as simply counting calories or tallying fat grams, it's time to think about food in a new way. Eating well means enjoying great taste as well as great nutrition. No single food provides all of the nutrients your body needs. Eating a variety of foods helps ensure the right mix of nutrients for good health.

The basics

Experts agree that the best way to increase nutrients in your diet and limit fat and calories is to eat more plant-based foods. Plant foods — fruits, vegetables and foods made from whole grains — contain beneficial vitamins, minerals, fibers and health-enhancing compounds called phytochemicals. By emphasizing plant foods in your diet, you increase consumption of many naturally healthy compounds.

For good health and better success at controlling your weight, here are the types and amounts of foods to eat each day. The recommendations are

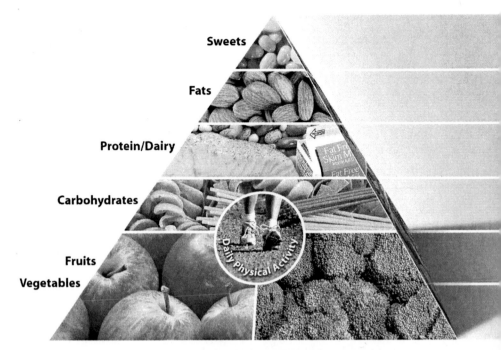

Mayo Clinic Healthy Weight Pyramid

based on the Mayo Clinic Healthy Weight Pyramid — a healthy eating plan for all Americans.

Vegetables: Unlimited servings. Vegetables are naturally low in calories, and almost all are fat-free. They provide vitamins, minerals and fiber. They also contain phytochemicals.

Fresh vegetables are best, but frozen vegetables are good, too. Most canned vegetables are high in sodium, which is used as a preservative in the canning process. Excessive sodium can increase blood pressure in some people. If you eat canned vegetables, select those with a label indicating that no sodium has been added.

Fruits: Unlimited servings. Fruit is generally low in calories and contains little or no fat. Fruit also contains many beneficial nutrients and phytochemicals.

Fresh fruit is always best. It makes a great snack. If you get the urge to snack between meals or you have a sweet tooth, keep a bowl of fresh fruit nearby. Frozen fruits with no added sugar and fruits canned in water or their own juices are acceptable alternatives. Eat dried fruits, such as dates and prunes, sparingly because they're a concentrated source of calories. Fruit juice also is a concentrated source of calories.

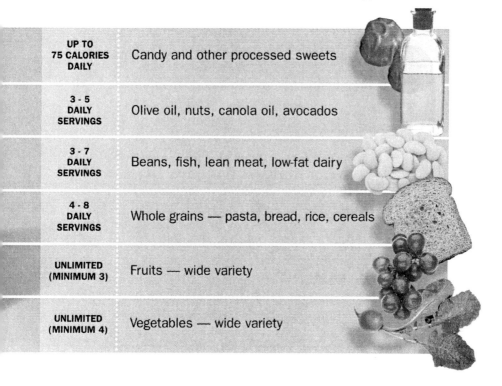

UP TO 75 CALORIES DAILY	Candy and other processed sweets
3 - 5 DAILY SERVINGS	Olive oil, nuts, canola oil, avocados
3 - 7 DAILY SERVINGS	Beans, fish, lean meat, low-fat dairy
4 - 8 DAILY SERVINGS	Whole grains — pasta, bread, rice, cereals
UNLIMITED (MINIMUM 3)	Fruits — wide variety
UNLIMITED (MINIMUM 4)	Vegetables — wide variety

Avocados, which are technically fruits, contain considerable calories and fat, and their use should be limited.

Carbohydrates: 4 to 8 servings. Carbohydrates include grain products, such as cereals, breads, rice and pasta, and starchy vegetables, such as corn, potatoes and some types of squash.

Along with vegetables and fruits, carbohydrates should form the foundation of your daily diet. Whenever possible, select whole-grain foods over refined products. Whole grains contain bran and germ, which add fiber. Whole grains are also important sources of vitamins and minerals.

Some carbohydrates, such as croissants, crackers and dessert breads, are high in fat and calories. But most plain cereals, breads and pasta are low in fat and calories. It's what you put on these foods — whole milk, cream, or spreads and sauces made from fats, oils or cheese — that adds calories.

Protein/Dairy: 3 to 7 servings. Protein is an essential nutrient that helps maintain body tissues, such as skin, bone and muscle. Protein is found in a variety of foods, including milk, yogurt, cheese, eggs, meat, poultry, fish and legumes (beans, dried peas and lentils). Most Americans eat far more protein than they need, especially those products that are high in fat and calories, such as meat.

Two to three of your daily protein servings should come from low-fat or fat-free milk or milk products (yogurt and cheese). Milk, yogurt and cheese are major sources of calcium and vitamin D. Calcium helps keep your bones healthy and reduces your risk of osteoporosis, a disease that reduces bone density and makes your bones brittle. Having arthritis puts you at increased risk of osteoporosis (see page 70).

Always try to select fat-free or low-fat varieties of protein, such as poultry (without skin), fish, lean meats, skim milk and low-fat cheeses. Plant proteins, such as legumes, are also excellent sources of protein.

Fats: 3 to 5 servings. A small amount of fat in your diet is necessary to help your body function, but most people consume far more than they need. Foods high in fat include products produced mainly from oils, butter, margarine, salad dressing or mayonnaise. An easy way to reduce fat in your diet is to reduce the amount of oil, butter and margarine you add to food when preparing it. Many snack products, such as chips and crackers, are also high in fat.

Healthier fats include those that contain monounsaturated fat, such as olive oil and canola oil. But even these should be eaten sparingly.

Sweets: Up to 75 calories daily. Sweets such as candy and desserts contain considerable calories, and they offer little in terms of nutrition. Many sweets are also high in fat. You don't have to give up sweets entirely to eat healthy, but be smart about your selections and portion sizes. Instead of sugar-sweetened soft drinks, candy bars or pastries, consider healthier choices, such as water, fresh fruit, low-fat frozen yogurt, angel food cake or reduced-calorie cookies.

Determining your servings for a healthy weight

The Mayo Clinic Healthy Weight Pyramid provides a range of servings for each food group. The number of servings you should eat within each range depends on a variety of factors, including your weight, activity level, age and whether you want to lose weight. If you're trying to lose weight, you'll want to aim for the lower number of servings in the food groups rather than the higher number. It's important, however, that you eat at least the minimum servings for each food group to maintain good health. A dietitian can help you determine how many servings of each food you should eat to maintain a calorie level that will help you lose weight.

As you adopt a healthier diet, it's also important to understand what constitutes a serving (see "Sizing up a serving"). With the trend toward supersizing, mega-buffets and huge portions in restaurants, many people have an inaccurate idea of what a regular portion is. Pay close

Sizing up a serving

Here are examples of what counts as one serving:

Grains
½ cup (3 oz/90 g) cooked cereal, rice or pasta
½ cup (1 oz/30 g) ready-to-eat cereal
1 4-inch (10-cm) pancake
1 slice whole-wheat (whole-meal) sandwich bread
½ bagel or English muffin
2 cups air-popped popcorn

Vegetables and fruits
2 cups (2 oz/60 g) raw leafy green vegetables
½ cup (3 oz/90 g) cooked vegetables
1 medium potato
½ cup (3 oz/90 g) applesauce
¼ cup (1½ oz/45 g) raisins
½ cup (6 fl oz/180 mL) 100% fruit juice
1 small apple or banana

Dairy products
1 cup (8 fl oz/250 mL) low-fat or fat-free milk or yogurt
1½ oz (45 g) reduced-fat or fat-free cheese
⅔ cup (6 oz/180 g) low-fat or nonfat cottage cheese

Poultry, seafood, meat
2-3 oz (60-90 g) cooked skinless poultry, seafood or lean meat

Meat alternatives
Each of these counts as 1 oz (30 g) of meat:
  ½ cup (3½ oz/105 g) cooked legumes
1 egg
2 tbsp peanut butter
¼ cup (1 oz/30 g) seeds
⅓ cup (1 oz/30 g) nuts
½ cup (4 oz/125 g) tofu

attention to portion sizes. Don't just estimate. Practice at home by actually measuring and weighing cupfuls and spoonfuls.

Menu planning

Many people say they don't plan menus, but everyone plans, if only for what to pick up at the grocery store. Planning menus means thinking about what foods to eat for a meal, a day or a week. There are many advantages to planning meals, and you don't have to lock yourself into a rigid schedule. Planning has these advantages:

Increases variety. You can include new foods and vary the colors, textures, flavors and shapes of foods to make meals attractive and interesting. Planning can make it easier to choose foods that are low in fat and calories and high in nutrients.

Although a nutritionally balanced diet is ideal, it may be unrealistic if you have limited mobility. Regardless of how many calories you eat, if your diet regularly falls short in one or more of the food groups, talk to your doctor or registered dietitian. A daily vitamin, mineral or meal supplement may be necessary.

Saves energy and money. When you go to the grocery store, take advantage of pre-cut fruits and vegetables, meats cut for stir-frys and other items that can save you time in the kitchen. They may cost a little more, but they're worth it when your energy is low or you're in pain. Even prepared foods from the grocery store are less expensive than take-out or restaurant foods of similar nutritional value.

Saves time and effort. Needed items will be on hand, which means fewer trips to the grocery store. You can also make good use of leftovers, which can decrease preparation time and effort.

Cooking with ease

The time you have to prepare a meal and the amount of preparation you're able to manage are major factors in deciding what foods to serve.

Make use of energy-saving storage devices such as Lazy Susans and pegboards and buy easy-open containers to keep food and equipment handy. A small cart on wheels can save a lot of steps and energy. Use it to set and clear the table. Arrange one complete place setting at a time and work your way around the table. Use the cart to carry items back to the sink, or have family members carry, scrape and stack their own dishes.

If you immediately rinse all cooking utensils and equipment after use, you won't have as

Adding nutrition to convenience foods

Here are some easy nutritional fixes for convenience foods:

- Add fresh peppers, grated carrots, mushrooms and onions to canned spaghetti sauce to boost fiber and nutrients.
- Top frozen pizza with fresh tomatoes and your favorite vegetables before heating.
- When preparing packaged rice, toss in vegetables (peas, broccoli, corn) or fruit (raisins, apple, apricots).
- Serve fresh fruits and vegetables as extra side dishes when eating frozen microwave dinners.
- Add a bag of ready-to-eat leafy salad greens and a loaf of crusty whole-grain bread the next time you opt for deli foods.

much scrubbing to do later. A small electric food processor is easy to clean and can effortlessly chop and dice foods and grate cheese. Use cooking utensils you can put in your dishwasher.

When cooking, try these work-simplification techniques:
- Study and improve placement of utensils to save steps and motions.
- Gather utensils and necessary items from storage areas and the refrigerator using a cart.
- Slide heavy objects along the counter rather than lift them.
- Serve hot items from the stove rather than lift heavy pots and pans.
- Cook and serve in the same dish whenever possible.
- Use a slotted spoon to remove vegetables from water.
- Place a nonslip pad or wet cloth under a mixing bowl to help hold it stationary without gripping.
- Work on paper towels when preparing vegetables and fruits to ease the cleanup.
- Keep knives sharpened.

Plan to have leftovers to freeze and heat at another time or that can be quickly served in a new way. For example, a roast can be used later in the week for a stir-fry meal or added to salad greens for lunch. Make a double batch of a casserole. Keep one in the freezer for a day when you're too tired to cook.

Eating out

When you eat out, don't let large portions, unfamiliar menus and tempting desserts discourage you from your commitment to healthy eating.

Here are key points to keep in mind:

Look carefully for your restaurant. Find a restaurant that offers a variety of foods, so you're not pressured into having what your companions order. Establishments that prepare the food you order from start to finish are more likely to accommodate special requests. A telephone call ahead of time (during nonpeak restaurant hours) can help you choose a restaurant best suited to your needs.

Keep hunger under control. Don't skip a meal on a day you're eating out. In fact, you may want to have a light snack an hour or so before the meal to avoid overeating.

Restaurant portion control

How many calories and how much fat do you avoid when you cut the portion sizes of these restaurant foods by half?

Food	Original portion	Original calories/ fat (grams)	Calories and fat (grams) saved by having ½ portion
Butter or margarine	2 pats	70/8	35/4
Salad dressing	1 ladle (4 tbsp)	280/28	140/14
Tartar sauce	4 tbsp	280/32	140/16
Roasted chicken breast	8 oz	325/8	162/4
Sirloin steak	12 oz	1,120/88	560/44
Prime rib	12 oz	1,440/124	720/62
Fish fillet (breaded and batter fried)	8 oz	530/30	265/15

Survey the selections. Many restaurants have special listings for healthy eating. However, foods in the diet or light section may have far more calories and fat than you might expect. Look for meals that contain little or no fat, small amounts of meat, poultry or fish, and lots of vegetables and low-fat carbohydrates, such as baked potato, rice or bread.

Order wisely. Ordering a la carte can be more expensive, but it lets you get just what you want. It has the advantage of variety and reduced quantity. Try making a meal out of broth-based (not creamed) soup or a salad and one appetizer. Look for appetizers that are broiled, baked or steamed, not fried. In addition, consider sharing a meal, or ask for a take-home box to come with your food, so you can immediately remove half to take home for another time.

Speak up. Ask your server to clarify unfamiliar terms or to explain how a dish is prepared. Request smaller portions and substitutions such as fresh fruit for french fries, dressings and sauces on the side and dry broiling (not basted with oil or fat) instead of frying.

Cut out the condiments. Taste your food before instinctively adding salt, butter, sauces and dressing. Well-prepared food needs minimal enhancement. Ask for sauces or dressing on the side. Then use the fork-dip-food technique. Dab your fork in the sauce and then pick up your food. This allows you to enjoy the sauce but limits the amount.

Special nutrition issues

Do foods such as red meat, citrus fruits, tomatoes (and other nightshade foods containing glycoalkaloids), aspartame and alfalfa sprouts aggravate rheumatic conditions? Questions such as this are frequently asked by people with arthritis. Because the symptoms of arthritis vary from day to day, it seems natural to think that what you eat might affect how you feel.

No scientific evidence shows that any particular food makes joint pain or inflammation better or worse. If you believe a particular food increases your symptoms, it's probably OK to omit that food from your diet. However, don't omit whole food groups or a large number of foods without first consulting a registered dietitian or your doctor.

There are special nutrition-related issues that do affect individuals with both rheumatoid arthritis and osteoarthritis.

10 ways to spot junk claims about nutrition
Members of the Food and Nutrition Science Alliance (FANSA) offer these tips to help you evaluate information about healthy eating. Any of the following signs should raise a warning flag:
1. Recommendations that promise a quick fix
2. Dire warnings of danger from a single product or regimen
3. Claims that sound too good to be true
4. Simplistic conclusions drawn from a complex study
5. Recommendations based on a single study
6. Dramatic statements that are refuted by reputable scientific organizations
7. Lists of "good" and "bad" foods
8. Recommendations made to help sell a product
9. Recommendations based on studies that are published without first being reviewed by experts
10. Recommendations from studies that ignore differences among individuals or groups

Alternative diets and supplements

If you have arthritis, you may wonder about the helpfulness of particular foods, diets or supplements touted to improve your symptoms. Because the symptoms of arthritis can change daily, it's easy to assume that what you ate or drank had an effect on how you feel.

Researchers are investigating the effects of low-calorie, low-fat and low-protein eating plans. Other scientists are looking at the benefits and risks of omega-3 fatty acids from cold-water fish (salmon, mackerel, herring) or plant (flax) oils to reduce joint tenderness. Research also is under way to determine whether diet affects the immune system, which causes the swelling and soreness of certain types of arthritis.

Remember that most claims about special diets and supplements for arthritis have no scientific basis. It's important to check with your doctor before taking any supplement or drastically changing your regular diet. (See Chapter 9 for more information.)

Benefits of a healthy weight

Whether you have osteoarthritis or rheumatoid arthritis, if you're carrying extra weight, weight reduction can reduce stress on your back, hips, knees and feet — all places where you may feel pain. Obesity clearly makes the symptoms of arthritis worse. Weight loss is especially important if you and your doctor are considering joint surgery, because excess weight can make the procedure more difficult and risky. In fact, some surgeons insist that their overweight patients lose weight before they undergo elective operations.

Excess weight adds stress to your weight-bearing joints, worsening pain, stiffness and inflammation. A decrease of just 5 percent to 10 percent in weight may:

- Decrease pain
- Increase mobility
- Increase energy level
- Decrease fatigue
- Improve self-image
- Provide a sense of control
- Increase ability to exercise
- Improve balance, which may prevent falls

The adage "You are what you eat" is only partially true. Other factors play a role as well:

Food intake. Your intake of calories and the number of calories your body needs for energy (calories burned) influence your weight. If calorie consumption from foods is greater than your energy needs, weight gain will occur over time.

Body composition. Lean muscle mass is your fat-free body weight. Lean muscle mass is important because it helps you burn more calories, making weight control easier. Exercise is the only proven method of increasing lean muscle tissue.

Calories are burned through activity. If the number of calories you eat is less than your energy needs, the result will be weight loss. Try to keep active. Inactivity results in weight gain — if your food intake remains constant — which may in turn cause further pain. This can lead to more inactivity and result in a cycle of weight gain that is difficult to break.

Eating well can help you control weight, but adding regular moderate physical activity is just as important. Even with arthritis, there are many activities to choose from that can help burn calories and increase muscle mass. Normal daily activities such as cleaning, shopping and doing laundry help burn calories too. Strengthening exercises, such as weight training, counteract muscle loss due to aging. The more active you are, the easier it is to maintain and even increase your muscle mass and keep a healthy weight. (See Chapter 3 for more information on exercise.) On days when you're not feeling well, try to choose lower intensity activities.

Mix and match for better health

Spending just 30 to 40 minutes in any combination of these activities burns about 200 calories. Try to be this active on most days.

Activity	Calories burned in 10 minutes of activity*
Light housework (polishing furniture)	20 to 25
Strolling (1 mph)	20 to 25
Golfing, with a motorized cart	25 to 40
Ballroom dancing	30 to 60
Walking at a brisk pace	50 to 60
Golfing, without a motorized cart	50 to 60
Leisurely bike riding	60 to 70
Swimming, slow crawl	80 to 90

*Calories are based on a 150-pound person. If you weigh less than 150 pounds, you need to spend more time to use up the same number of calories. Weighing more than 150 pounds means you use up the same number of calories in less time.

Calcium and osteoporosis

If your arthritis causes extended periods of inactivity, you may have an increased risk of developing osteoporosis, the "brittle bones" disease, because inactivity can lead to calcium loss from bone. Each year, more than 1.5 million Americans have fractures related to osteoporosis.

Getting enough calcium in your diet may help slow bone loss and reduce your risk of osteoporosis. In addition, you also need vitamin D to enhance the amount of calcium that ultimately reaches your bones. Your body makes vitamin D when sunlight converts a chemical in your skin into a usable form of this nutrient. Supplements may be appropriate for people who don't get enough calcium and vitamin D in food, who live in cloudy environments or who rarely go outside.

The recommended intakes for calcium and vitamin D are listed below. Although it's best to meet your needs for these bone-saving nutrients with a well-chosen diet, many people fail to do so. It's important to include at least two servings of high-calcium foods every day. If you frequently miss this mark, check with your doctor or registered dietitian about the need for supplemental calcium and vitamin D.

Regular weight-bearing exercise such as walking or strength training also helps keep bones strong. And if you're a postmenopausal woman, estrogen replacement in combination with exercise and adequate dietary calcium offers the best defense against bone loss and fractures.

Medications for osteoporosis

In addition to dietary measures, several medications are available to promote stronger bones. Hormone replacement therapy with estrogens, often referred to as HRT, is widely used by women after menopause. Raloxifene (Evista) adjusts the action of estrogens on cells of your body. Calcitonin (Miacalcin) is another hormone that acts on bone. It's usually

Daily calcium and vitamin D recommendations for men and women

Age (years)	Calcium (mg)	Vitamin D (IU)
19 to 50	1,000	200
51 to 70	1,200	400
71 and older	1,200	600

15 best sources of calcium

Along with 3 cups of milk, a serving or two of any of these foods will provide more than 1,000 milligrams (mg) of daily calcium.

Food	Calcium (mg)
Milk (skim and low-fat), 1 cup	300
Rice (calcium-fortified), 1 cup	300
Tofu set with calcium, ½ cup	260
Yogurt, 1 cup (average of low-fat brands)	250
Orange juice (calcium-fortified), 1 cup	240
Ready-to-eat cereal (calcium-fortified), 1 cup	200
Mozzarella cheese (part-skim), 1 oz	185
Canned salmon with bones, 3 oz	180
Collards, ½ cup cooked	180
Ricotta cheese (part skim), ¼ cup	170
Bread (calcium-fortified), 2 slices	160
Cottage cheese (1% fat), 1 cup	140
Parmesan cheese, 2 tbsp	140
Navy beans, 1 cup cooked	130
Turnips, ½ cup cooked	125

given by intra-nasal spray. Alendronate (Fosamax) and risedronate (Actonel) are bisphosphonates that inhibit bone loss.

Food and drug interactions

Just as the foods you eat can alter the effectiveness of some medications, some medications can interfere with how well your body uses nutrients. You may need higher-than-usual amounts of certain vitamins or minerals, depending on the medications you're taking. Often you can choose foods that provide the extra nutrients you need. Sometimes your doctor may recommend a supplement.

How and when to take your medication should be thoroughly understood. Some of the drugs used to treat arthritis and its symptoms are most effective if you take them on an empty stomach, but others should be taken with food to prevent stomach irritation. Carefully follow the instructions of your doctor and pharmacist.

Some of the most common side effects of arthritis medications include heartburn and an upset stomach, often described as a gnawing pain or empty feeling in the stomach. These symptoms can be caused by food, medication or a combination of both. Sit upright for at least 15 to 30 minutes after meals and taking medications. Try to avoid eating for at least 1 hour before bedtime. Limit foods that tend to trigger reactions, such as alcohol, caffeine, colas, spicy foods, fried foods and pepper.

Appetite control

The long-term use of particular drugs may increase your appetite, making it more difficult to keep your weight under control. Eat slowly and stretch mealtimes to a minimum of 20 to 30 minutes to allow your natural appetite control mechanism to work. Increasing the amount of high-fiber foods can help you feel full sooner. Try whole-grain breads instead of white bread, fresh fruit instead of juice, and raw vegetables in place of cooked vegetables for added fiber.

Try these additional tips to help appease an overactive appetite:

Eat breakfast. Eating regular meals and snacks prevents the "famine-then-feast" syndrome. Make breakfast a high-fiber cereal, whole-grain bread and fresh fruit, and you may feel less tempted to eat fatty, sugary snacks in the morning. It can also set you up for eating a more balanced lunch.

Be sure you're hungry. Are you eating because you're stressed or bored? Substitute reading, a physical activity or a phone call to a friend.

Eat slowly. Savor each flavor and texture to boost your satisfaction. Remember, it takes about 20 minutes for your brain to receive the signal that you're full. Make sure your meals last at least this long.

Ride out the urge. Cravings generally pass within minutes, maybe even seconds. Busy yourself with an activity unrelated to food until the desire to eat passes.

Start small. If you always finish what's in front of you, start with half the amount of food you usually eat on your plate. You may find smaller servings more satisfying. To make less food seem like more, serve your main course on a salad or dessert plate.

Enjoy a treat now and then. If you're really committed to eating less, an occasional lapse is OK. It has little impact on a lifetime plan for controlling your appetite.

Chapter 6

Your thoughts, feelings and beliefs and your health

Because your mind and body are integrally connected, your beliefs about yourself, your arthritis and life itself have a powerful influence on you and your health. Whether you're optimistic or pessimistic, whether you think you have control and whether you have confidence in yourself affect how you approach life and how well you cope.

Put simply, positive or optimistic thoughts and beliefs have health-enhancing benefits. Optimists are convinced they can make things work out. If you're an optimist, your positive attitude buffers you from stress because you react to adversity by taking action. You face life's slings and arrows with a sense of hope. But negative or pessimistic thoughts and beliefs can intensify your stress and pain and hamper your immune system. If you're a pessimist, you're at risk of depression and anxiety. And you may react by feeling helpless, not hopeful, when adversity strikes.

The mind-body connection works in many ways. First, if you believe you have control, you'll take better care of yourself, such as eating right, exercising and getting enough rest, than if you think nothing you do matters. Second, studies show that feelings of helplessness weaken the immune system by inhibiting the actions of T cells and natural killer cells, both of which attack invaders such as bacteria, viruses and tumor cells. Third, pessimistic people tend to isolate themselves, cutting themselves off from the proven health-enhancing benefits of friendship, love and support.

For arthritis in particular, research indicates that how you fare depends at least as much on your own actions as on those of your doctor and other health professionals. If you believe you can manage your arthritis — if you believe you can gain control over your pain and fatigue — then you're more likely to use medical resources more effectively than are people who have no faith in their ability to fight the disease. In fact, if you and someone else have the same degree of physical impairment and you have better coping skills, you're likely to experience less pain and have less difficulty functioning.

It has taken years of research for science to prove what you learned as a child. If, like Chicken Little, you believe the sky will fall, you can subject your body to a constant state of damaging stress, increase your feelings of helplessness and make your day-to-day existence more difficult. But if, like the Little Engine That Could, you believe in yourself and your abilities, you can accomplish amazing things, such as managing your arthritis and living a full and satisfying life despite it. The choice is yours.

The healer within

Psychoneuroimmunology (si-ko-noor-o-imu-NOL-o-je) is a field of study concerned with the interplay among stress, emotions, the nervous system, immune functions and disease. Your immune system's job is to maintain your health and facilitate healing by warding off invaders, such as viruses, and battling abnormal cells. Your nervous system influences immune functioning by connecting nerves to your spleen, lymph nodes and thymus — organs that are part of the immune system — and through the release of hormones.

When you're stressed, your body gears up to either fight or flee by triggering areas of your brain to release hormones into your bloodstream. You know the feeling. When you're scared or excited, your heart beats faster, your breathing speeds up, your blood pressure increases and your muscles tense. Those reactions can give you the boost you need to pass a test or give a speech. But there's a downside. Research shows that chemicals released during stressful times can suppress your immune system, making you more susceptible to illness.

When you have a chronic condition such as arthritis, stress can make it harder for you to deal with challenges. Perhaps one of the worst effects of stress is that the resulting muscle tension can worsen your pain, which may limit your abilities, cause you to feel helpless and intensify other feelings you might have, such as anger, anxiety, annoyance or frustration. As a result, you might become depressed, which makes you feel more helpless, setting up a painful cycle.

Stress is simply part of life, and you have no control over many stressful occurrences, such as the death of a loved one. Even positive events, such as a promotion or a wedding, cause stress. For most of us, however, minor stressors are more common than major events. Research has shown that these minor events play a significant role in how you feel day to day. But stress also comes from within, and it's how you react to external situations that determines the level of stress you experience. Fortunately, you can learn to manage your stress.

Listening to your body

The first step in breaking the cycle — stress, increased pain, decreased abilities and depression — is learning to recognize when you're under stress. People experience stress differently. Here are common signs and symptoms:

- Fatigue
- Muscle tension and pain
- Anxiety
- Irritability
- Temper outbursts
- Stomach upset
- Sleep disturbances
- Changes in appetite
- Headache
- Cold, sweaty palms
- Teeth grinding or jaw clenching

If you develop any of these, first be sure they're not caused by something else, such as the flu. Once you determine, possibly with the help of your doctor, that your symptoms are indeed stress-related, you need to figure out what's causing them. Obviously, situations such as divorce or a death in the family are major stressors. But what about the day-to-day occurrences that rev up your stress reactors?

Take note of things that make your heart beat faster and boost your blood pressure. Is it fighting with your teenager, sitting in rush-hour traffic, juggling too many commitments or maybe all of these? Try keeping a stress diary for a few weeks to get a better handle on what sets your nerves on edge.

Once you identify your symptoms and what triggers them, you can begin to control your stress, either by changing the situation, if possible, or by altering your reaction to it.

Accentuate the positive

OK, so you have arthritis. That's no reason to think of yourself as unhealthy.

In *Minding the Body, Mending the Mind*, Joan Borysenko, a psychologist and cell biologist who specializes in mind-body medicine, writes of a former Olympic skier whose career was ended by multiple sclerosis (MS). First, he got depressed. Later, he realized he had choices: He could be a healthy person with MS or an unhealthy person with MS. He decided to exercise, eat well and meditate daily. He began to see himself as an extremely healthy person who happened to have MS.

How do you see yourself? You, too, have choices. Taking care of yourself, by eating the right foods, exercising and getting enough rest, will go a long way toward making you feel better and keeping you active. But what if you don't believe you have control over your situation? Chances are your automatic thoughts are working against you.

Rapid-fire or automatic thoughts pass through your brain constantly, although you're not aware of most of them. If you stop and attend to your thoughts for a moment, you might be surprised how negative your self-talk can be. For example, you start a walking program and instead of focusing on the good you're doing yourself, you chide yourself for being out of shape. Or, before you give a presentation at work, you tell yourself, "I can't," "I'm no good at this" or "They'll think I'm stupid." These are called automatic thoughts. Much stress comes from such negative thinking, which is usually unrealistic and distorted.

Psychologist Albert Ellis, the originator of rational-emotive therapy, said stress mostly develops not from what happens to us but from how we react to it. Our reactions are largely determined by irrational beliefs we hold, such as, "I should never make a mistake," "Everyone should like me," "It's always wrong to get angry." Notice the "should," "always" and "never." Developing more realistic expectations for yourself and others through modifying these irrational beliefs is a powerful way to reduce stress.

You have to make yourself aware of your beliefs about yourself and understand how they trigger automatic thoughts. Begin to pay attention to what you're telling yourself. In regard to your arthritis, do you find yourself asking, "Why me?" and telling yourself that life as you know it is over? When you catch yourself in the act of negative self-talk, stop, take a deep breath and think about the effect your thoughts are having on you. Use positive self-talk to tone down your critical or negative thinking. For example, instead of, "I'll never again be able to do the things I enjoy," tell yourself, "I'll take good care of myself so that I can still do many things" or "I may have to slow down, but I don't have to give up."

David Burns, M.D., a psychiatrist and clinical associate professor at the Stanford University School of Medicine, believes that moods, including depression, result from the way you think about events, not the events themselves. He recommends restructuring negative thinking by writing down your negative thoughts as they occur. When you do something you consider a personal failure, such as needing help opening a jar, write down the thoughts that go through your head. Then counter them with a defense. For example, if your thought is, "I'm always such a burden on everyone," replace it with a more objective, rational one, such as, "Some days are better than others. Today I need more help." Tell the truth because to change your reactions, you have to believe the rational thoughts. Dr. Burns suggests using this technique 15 minutes a day for several months to begin to replace automatic distortions with rational thinking.

Stress busting: Relaxation techniques

Besides restructuring stress-inducing thoughts, several other techniques can help you relax. As noted earlier, relaxing helps reduce the muscle tension that can increase pain. Finding a relaxation technique or techniques that work for you can help you decrease your pain and increase your peace of mind.

Relaxation techniques need to be learned, which means practicing them regularly. Yoga and other Eastern exercises involving defined postures and repetitive movements can help you relax. Prayer can be a form of meditation, especially when the prayer is simple, familiar and repetitive. These quiet, repetitive exercises can serve to reverse the mental arousal from stress. Regular practice also may provide new insights into how to reduce your stress by changing your priorities or thought patterns because these exercises serve as another powerful form of thought shifting.

A family matter

My three young sons and I all have rheumatoid arthritis. My wife, Nicki, is the only one in the family without the disease.

I've had arthritis since I was 6 weeks old. A swollen left elbow was the first clue. Thirty years later this was also the first clue for our oldest son, Timothy, when he was 3 months of age. He's now 8. Our twins, Jacob and Paul, developed the symptoms when they were 1. They're now 5.

Sometimes at our house, stress soars off the scale. It can happen in the morning when we're struggling to get one of the boys ready to go to the doctor to have swollen joints drained or injected with steroids. It can be hard to find the energy for patience when you've been up all night with them, soaking their flaring joints. But sometimes even those nights become divine, as we sit in the hot tub under the starlight and talk for hours about everything from knock-knock jokes to why Timothy can't play soccer anymore and how his courage inspires Mom and me.

We cope with the stresses. When there are a lot of swellings going on and things start to get crazy, we back away from activities. Timothy hasn't been to Cub Scouts much this year, and he didn't make it to soccer, although we paid the $50 fee — just in case. We often, at the last minute, have to cancel holiday gatherings with family and friends. We've taken Timothy to counseling to help him over the depression he felt. Nicki and I also go to counseling to keep our marriage strong enough to endure the stresses created by the arthritis. Our friends have been a great help, too, watching the kids and running errands. Once, during an especially tough time, they brought meals for 3 months.

Nicki has a unique way of looking at our family's arthritis. She says the disease has shaped me into a "positive, focused, creative, wonderful person." And she tells our boys that it can do the same for them, if they decide to journey with arthritis instead of thinking of themselves as victims. For victims can only grow bitter, but travelers grow stronger each day.

Kevin
Arlington, Texas

Here's a look at some of the more common techniques. For massage, you'll need to find an expert. You can learn self-hypnosis, but probably not by yourself. For the self-help techniques, you'll need to practice. There are many guided meditation and guided imagery tapes on the market which you may find helpful. Pick a quiet time and place where you won't be disturbed. Practice regularly, preferably daily, for a minimum of 15 to 20 minutes. And be patient — it may take several weeks to get the hang of it and start to see some benefit.

Meditation. This has been called an altered state of consciousness and a unique state of relaxation. There are almost as many ways to meditate as there are people who meditate. The basic premise is to sit quietly and focus on nothing or on your breathing or on a simple word or phrase repeated over and over. When distracting thoughts arise — and they will — you simply notice them and let them go, always returning to your focus. With meditation, you enter a deeply restful state that reduces your body's stress response. Types of meditative practice include mindfulness meditation, the relaxation response and, the most studied, transcendental meditation. They work similarly. Regular practice of meditation can relax your breathing, slow brain waves and decrease muscle tension and heart rate. It can also lessen your body's response to the chemicals it produces when you're stressed, such as adrenaline, which can have harmful effects on your body.

Guided imagery (visualization). This is a technique in which you enter a relaxed state brought on by meditation or self-hypnosis. There you imagine an image you experience with your senses to help you alleviate physical symptoms. Studies of the brains of people engaged in guided imagery sessions suggest that the same parts of your brain are stimulated when you imagine something as when you actually experience it. The message your brain receives from your imagination is sent to other brain centers and to your body's autonomic and endocrine systems, which regulate key functions such as heart rate and blood pressure. This may be why worry — imagining the worst — can increase your blood pressure and cause your pulse to race and muscles to tense just as if the worst did happen.

Progressive muscle relaxation. This works on the theory that to learn how to relax your muscles, you must know how they feel tensed. Therefore, progressive relaxation is a series of exercises that takes you through each of the major muscle groups from head to toe — tensing and releasing tension as you go. Along the way, you focus on how the relaxed muscles feel compared with the tense muscles.

Another important phase of progressive muscle relaxation involves a technique called body scanning, in which you focus on each muscle group in turn, note any tension and then let it go without first tensing the muscles.

Hypnosis. This is an induced state of relaxation that enhances your focus and makes you more open to act on suggestions given to you — or that you give yourself — when you're in a hypnotic state. Hypnosis alters your brain-wave patterns in much the same way as other relaxation techniques. This stress-relieving ability may be why it works to ease pain and alter behavior. About 80 percent of adults can be hypnotized. Because, like narcotics, hypnosis can mask pain and, therefore, possibly cause you to injure your joints, hypnosis isn't usually recommended for people with arthritis. Self-hypnosis, however, is similar to some of the other techniques discussed here and may be valuable to you in managing stress and pain.

Massage therapy. This involves the manipulation of soft tissues of your body. It comes in many forms — from the traditional kneading and rubbing of Swedish massage to the application of pressure at the acupuncture points of the body, which characterizes shiatsu massage. This "healing touch" reduces your heart rate, increases circulation, relaxes muscles, improves range of motion and increases production of endorphins, which can relieve pain and anxiety. Massage is effective at relieving stress, depression and anxiety. It can also increase alertness and decrease pain perception. It has been shown to reduce arthritis pain. The environment in which you receive massage is important. A warm, quiet area, free from distracting noise or interruptions, can help relieve muscle tension. Low-volume sound or music also relaxes muscles. Your massage therapist should use a good lubricant, such as mineral oil. By reducing friction, the lubricant contributes to smooth, effective massage strokes. Don't have a massage if you have an open wound or skin infection. Check with your doctor if you've been injured.

Keep a journal. Writing down your thoughts and feelings can help you blow off steam, increase self-awareness, solve problems and put things in perspective. The Arthritis Foundation recommends keeping a journal. By doing so regularly, you can also create a record of your symptoms, see patterns in their occurrence, gain a better understanding of your disease, and find ways to communicate better with your doctors and others about your condition. According to the foundation, people with chronic illnesses who record their feelings often report fewer symptoms, fewer doctor visits, fewer days off work and improved moods.

Seeking support: You're not alone

Having friends and loved ones to talk to, especially when you're facing the pain and life changes arthritis imposes on you, can help you feel less alone and scared and more able to cope with your condition. Having people who care about you also makes you more likely to take better care of yourself. Beyond that, studies show that having support may lower your stress levels. Friends help protect you from the physical consequences of stress, and the more friends the better.

Research also shows that support groups offer similar benefits, with one possible advantage: In a group of relative strangers, you can express your deepest fears and daily concerns without worrying about scaring or burdening your loved ones. Depending on the nature of the group, you can deal with difficult problems, get help changing your perspective, share ideas and experiences and learn more about arthritis and how others facing the same challenges cope. To gain the most benefit from a group, however, you have to be willing to share your thoughts and feelings and be interested in learning about those of others. To find a group, talk to your doctor, your local Arthritis Foundation chapter or others you know who have arthritis.

If you're not comfortable being in a group but feel the need to express your feelings about your arthritis or want help learning cognitive restructuring or self-hypnosis, you might consider individual counseling. Talk to your doctor about recommending a therapist.

Simplifying your life

The last decade has brought with it a cultural phenomenon called voluntary simplicity. Proponents of voluntary simplicity seek to simplify their lives by scaling back on time commitments and material pursuits. Although you may not want to quit your job and move to the country, your arthritis may force you to slow down to allow more time for rest and self-care in your daily routine. In addition, you may want to pamper yourself by paying more attention to the things in your life that give you satisfaction and pleasure.

Mayo Clinic psychologist Barbara Bruce, Ph.D., offers these suggestions for simplifying your life:

Reassess success. Climbing the career ladder may not always be the right choice for you. You may make more money and have more prestige as a school principal, but is it worth the added stress and loss of pleasure you get from working with kids in a classroom? Making better use of your time and adding more meaning to your life may require giving up some clout to do the work you find rewarding. Is your job eating up too many hours of your day? Think about having more time — even if it means less money.

Accept the things you can't change. Maybe you can't do everything you did before you had arthritis. If you have rheumatoid arthritis, the wax-and-wane nature of your disease might make it difficult for you to plan, and you may be too tired to pursue every interest. Don't fight it. Decide what's important and assign priorities. Give those things you both must and want to do top priority. For the rest, delegate them, drop them or ask for help.

Take a breath. When you're rushed or stressed, your breathing is quick and shallow. Relaxed breathing is deep and slow. You can slow down by practicing deep breathing. Inhale slowly to a count of four, then exhale slowly to a count of four. Do this several times a day — whenever you're feeling rushed. Practice deep breathing when you're on hold, waiting in line or working on a deadline. Or let the ring of the telephone signal you to breathe deeply before you answer.

Practice saying no. You can't do everything, especially when you have arthritis. The next time someone asks for your help, think before you say yes. Do you have the time? Are you already overcommitted? Will you have to give up something else you want to do? Is this a project you really want to work on? Are you feeling overwhelmed or worn-out? There's no need to feel guilty; it's OK to say no. Besides, you won't be much use to anyone else if you're running on empty.

Own less, clean less. Unless it's edible, just about everything you bring into your house requires time- and energy-consuming maintenance. Perhaps you once enjoyed your figurine collection, but now you view it as a dust collection. Apply the "pleasure principle" to your possessions. Do they really make you happy? What would you take along if you had to evacuate your home in 1 hour? Consider getting rid of anything that doesn't significantly add to your life. If you haven't used it in a year, maybe you should put it in storage or give it away. And don't buy things you don't need.

The rest is rest

Throughout this chapter, we've looked at things you can do to gain control over your arthritis and enhance your quality of life. Certainly not the least of these is getting adequate rest. We live in a sleep-deprived culture in which achievement is valued over taking care of ourselves. For many, it's a source of pride not to need much sleep. More and more studies are showing the debilitating effects of sleep deprivation for the population in general. But for you, your arthritis makes it imperative that you listen to your body and give it what it needs, especially rest.

When should you rest? When you're tired. Arthritis, particularly rheumatoid arthritis, makes you more prone to fatigue. Know your limits. If you need to rest in a comfortable chair or nap during the day, do so. And be sure to get a good night's sleep. Sleep as many hours as you need, not as many as you think you should have. There are no prizes awarded for getting by on 4 hours a night, despite the culture, but you could aggravate your arthritis by not sleeping enough.

One caveat: It's possible to sleep too much. If you're depressed, you might seek refuge in sleep. Keep naps relatively short, especially if you find them interfering with your sleep at night. As an alternative to a nap, find a comfortable chair and rest without falling asleep. It's OK to be a little tired. And be sure to intersperse rest periods with periods of exercise and other activity.

You're in control

The term researchers have given to the belief that you can have control over things that affect your life is *self-efficacy.* Studies conducted at Stanford University show that self-efficacy — the ability to achieve intended results — is the best predictor of positive health outcomes in many situations, including who will cope well with arthritis. Achieving success, such as lessening your stress through one of the relaxation techniques, increases self-efficacy, as does seeing other people succeed in controlling the effects of their illness.

You can manage your arthritis. Throughout this chapter, we've looked at the power of your thoughts, feelings and beliefs about your illness and your life. We've offered many techniques that can help you gain control. In managing your arthritis, doing is believing.

For more information

Full Catastrophe Living: Using the Wisdom of Your Body and Mind to Face Stress, Pain and Illness, by Jon Kabat-Zinn, 1990

Learned Optimism: How to Change Your Mind and Your Life, by Martin Seligman, 1998.

Mind Body Medicine: How to Use Your Mind for Better Health, edited by Daniel Goleman and Joel Gurin, 1995.

Minding the Body, Mending the Mind, Joan Borysenko, 2000.

Timeshifting: Creating More Time to Enjoy Your Life, by Stephan Rechtschaffen, 1996.

Learning how to help yourself

The Arthritis Self-Help Course educates people about the different kinds of arthritis, teaches them how to exercise, explains the appropriate use of arthritis medications and stress management techniques, and encourages participants to take an active role in managing their condition.

Sponsored by the Arthritis Foundation, the course was developed in 1978. Since then, more than 100,000 people have completed it. On average, they report their pain reduced by 15 percent to 20 percent. They also report having less depression and making fewer medical visits after the course.

Follow-up studies show that participants tend to make the healthy behavior changes taught in the course, such as exercising. However, improvements in pain, depression and activity level are most closely linked to a positive adjustment in attitude. Course graduates are more confident that they can deal with their disease, as measured by psychological tests.

To find a course near you, contact your local Arthritis Foundation chapter or call the Arthritis Foundation at 800-283-7800.

Chapter 7

Medications for arthritis

Just as there's a spectrum of symptoms among people with rheumatoid arthritis and osteoarthritis — from minimal to severe — there's a broad spectrum of medications to help control the disease's pain and, in many cases, its damage. You and your doctor have many options.

Medications can help relieve your pain, help you increase activity or prevent further damage from inflammation. Some medications are relatively mild and sold without a prescription — common enough to be found for sale in convenience stores. Others are powerful prescription-only drugs.

The benefits of these drugs must be weighed against potentially dangerous side effects. They can help reduce pain and allow you a more active life, as long as they're taken with extreme care and attention to your doctor's instructions. Some drugs are used to treat several forms of arthritis, while others are used for a particular type.

If you have osteoarthritis, you can benefit from several drug therapies, particularly for the relief of pain. These medications include aspirin and related drugs, acetaminophen, other pain relievers and a few other types of medications.

In rheumatoid arthritis, the purpose of the medication is not only pain relief but also reduction of inflammation and the resulting potential for damage to the joints. Ideally, doctors and scientists hope to reduce the symptoms by controlling the underlying immune system abnormalities that lead to disease symptoms in the first place.

Also, controlling inflammation is one of the keys to reducing pain and getting you back into the lifestyle you want to pursue.

There are five primary groups of medications that doctors recommend for rheumatoid arthritis. Some are available for over-the-counter (OTC) purchase. Most, however, are prescription drugs:

- Nonsteroidal anti-inflammatory drugs (NSAIDs), including aspirin
- Corticosteroids, also called glucocorticoids
- Disease-modifying antirheumatic drugs (DMARDs), or remittive drugs
- Immunosuppressant drugs
- Biologic agents

Other drugs also can be used to treat arthritis. For example, topical creams can provide some pain relief. And acetaminophen is an effective pain reliever that may be among the safest drugs used by people with arthritis. Antidepressants also can be helpful.

NSAIDs

Suppressing inflammation is important in the treatment of rheumatoid arthritis because of the damage that inflammation may cause. By controlling inflammation, you also can reduce pain. However, NSAIDs (N-SAIDS) don't cure the disease. In rheumatoid arthritis, other medications usually are used with NSAIDs to control the disease.

If you have osteoarthritis, though, an anti-inflammatory drug isn't as likely to be necessary. That's because osteoarthritis — however painful — involves minimal inflammation. In fact, inflammation may be involved only in some phases of osteoarthritis.

There are two main categories of anti-inflammatory medications used by people with arthritis. One contains cortisone, or cortisone-related substances, such as prednisone, derived from human hormones. These substances can control inflammation effectively. However, if you take this type of medication for a long period, cortisone may produce serious side effects.

The other category of anti-inflammatory drugs has no cortisone. These medications go by the name nonsteroidal anti-inflammatory drugs — NSAIDs. They range from the most widely used drug in the world — aspirin — to ibuprofen to many more potent NSAIDs available only with a prescription.

These drugs are divided into two groups: the traditional NSAIDs such as ibuprofen and naproxen, and the newer COX-2 inhibitors such as celocoxib and rofecoxib.

How NSAIDs work

NSAIDs actually perform two primary beneficial functions.

Certain NSAIDs — such as aspirin, buffered aspirin and ibuprofen — are used for relief of everyday pain. If you have osteoarthritis, you can take NSAIDs in small doses to reduce pain. These painkillers (analgesics) also help eliminate other minor aches and pains, such as headaches and menstrual cramps.

If you have rheumatoid arthritis, NSAIDs are valuable because of their ability to reduce inflammation and its painful effects. Despite minor differences between types of NSAIDs, they work against inflammation in a similar way. NSAIDs inhibit an enzyme (cyclooxygenase) that promotes the production of prostaglandins — chemicals in the blood and tissues that are a key to the process of inflammation.

Because every person with arthritis is different, the best choice of NSAID varies from individual to individual. What works for you may not work for your best friend, and vice versa. That's why you and your doctor will choose an NSAID on the basis of several criteria:
- Your age and state of health
- The frequency of medication needed
- How you respond to a medication
- How your other medications may interact with the NSAID
- The cost of medications

There are many NSAID options for arthritis medication, both prescription and OTC. Like all NSAIDs, they need to be taken with respect to their potency if used at length, even aspirin. They have the capacity to produce serious and potentially dangerous side effects — gastric ulcers and bleeding.

Over-the-counter NSAIDs

Aspirin and its variants come in a trio of forms — plain, buffered and enteric coated. The buffered and enteric-coated types reduce potential

---

Generic vs. brand name

Many drugs used for treating arthritis are available as both brand-name and generic medications. What are the differences?

A drug that's discovered or developed in a laboratory begins with a generic name selected by experts and governmental agencies. Then the company that developed it typically gives it a brand name and sells it exclusively for a fixed period. When patent rights expire, any other drug company can manufacture and sell the drug under its generic name or another brand name. In any case, the Food and Drug Administration must approve it.

Generic drugs are available for about half of all drugs on the market. For consumers, that's generally good news because generics can cost considerably less than their brand-name counterparts.

You, your doctor and pharmacist must determine whether you should use a brand-name medication or a generic equivalent, based on your medical needs and your ability to afford the medication.

---

stomach irritation and acidity. Some common OTC brand-name aspirins include Bayer and Bufferin. Many generic forms are also available.

A relatively small dose of aspirin usually suffices for everyday pain relief (two 325-milligram tablets every 4 hours). That's how someone with osteoarthritis might use it.

Aspirin is used much less today to treat rheumatoid arthritis pain. But if you do use it for rheumatoid arthritis, you must keep a steady and substantial amount of aspirin in your bloodstream — up to 12 ordinary aspirin tablets a day. You can't approach it in the manner of taking a painkiller for a headache — using it only when the pain is occurring.

Besides aspirin and related medications, three other NSAIDs are available in nonprescription strengths. They can provide alternatives, in case you can't tolerate aspirin or it fails to do the job for you.

• Ibuprofen (Advil, Motrin IB, others)
• Ketoprofen (Orudis KT)
• Naproxen sodium (Aleve)

The cautions to be applied to use of these OTC NSAIDs are the same as those for aspirin. It's fine to use them for relief of minor pain without consulting a doctor. But if you're thinking about trying them on your own for your rheumatoid arthritis, think again. Take them only as directed by your physician.

Prescription NSAIDs

Many NSAIDs are available only with a doctor's prescription, including medications that contain aspirin. In general, they're stronger per dose than aspirin and other OTC drugs.

A few of these prescription NSAIDs come with a special benefit compared with other NSAIDs: You don't have to swallow a dozen pills at certain intervals throughout your day. You may need to take only one or two pills a day.

Beyond their convenience for busy people, these pills can help ensure that you take your medication properly. After all, sometimes it's hard to remember to take all of the pills that a regimen of aspirin requires. And compliance with your doctor's directions is vital.

Some one-a-day NSAIDs include:
• Diclofenac sodium (Voltaren)
• Ketoprofen (Oruvail)
• Nabumetone (Relafen)
• Naproxen (Naprelan)
• Etodolac (Lodine)
• Piroxicam (Feldene)
• Meloxicam (Mobic)

With some other prescription NSAIDs, you must take more than one pill a day. But you won't use the number of pills that a regimen of aspirin would require. Here are some examples:
• Diclofenac sodium and misoprostol (Arthrotec) — one tablet two to three times a day
• Ketoprofen (Orudis) — one capsule two to four times a day
• Naproxen (Naprosyn) — one tablet twice a day
• Fenoprofen (Nalfon) — one or two capsules three to four times a day
• Sulindac (Clinoril) — one tablet twice a day
• Flurbiprofen (Ansaid) — one tablet two to four times a day
• Indomethacin (Indocin) — one capsule two to three times a day
•Tolmetin (Tolectin) — one tablet three times a day

In addition, these and other prescription NSAIDs provide a spectrum of anti-inflammation alternatives. If you can't tolerate aspirin or find that it just doesn't help you, you and your doctor will want to try other options.

NSAID side effects

Most people who use NSAIDs for their arthritis don't have problems, or they have minor side effects that resolve themselves. Several may occur when you start using NSAIDs, such as the following:

- Mild headache
- Lightheadedness
- Drowsiness
- Dizziness

These side effects are apt to cease within a week or two. If they don't, tell your doctor. Ringing or noise in your ears (tinnitus) may occur if you're using aspirin or a related medication.

If you're using large doses of NSAIDs, there are more serious side effects that you should be aware of. By reducing the production of prostaglandins — which lead to creating inflammation — NSAIDs can interfere with their other, healthful functions. This can result in the following:

- Stomach and intestinal irritation
- Gastrointestinal bleeding
- Decreased kidney function
- Fluid retention
- Heart failure

Risks of adverse side effects are increased in older adults, especially women. If you have had stomach ulcers, gastrointestinal bleeding or kidney failure or if you're taking a blood thinner (anticoagulant), your doctor probably won't recommend traditional NSAIDs. Other side effects may occur, but they are less common. If you have questions about symptoms that develop while taking an NSAID, talk with your doctor.

Nonacetylated salicylates are related to aspirin, but they tend to be gentler to the stomach and kidneys. In addition, they have only a minimal effect on the promotion of bleeding — a common side effect of NSAIDs. Prescription nonacetylated salicylates include choline magnesium trisalicylate (Trilisate) and salsalate (Disalcid).

COX-2 inhibitors

This class of medications is similar to NSAIDs, but the drugs work in a different manner, reducing some of the side effects associated with traditional NSAIDs.

Like NSAIDs, COX-2 inhibitors block the production of an enzyme called cyclooxygenase (COX). Cyclooxygenase produces hormone-like substances called prostaglandins that trigger inflammation and pain. But unlike NSAIDs, COX-2 inhibitors mainly affect only one form of the enzyme instead of both.

In the early 1990s, researchers discovered that there are two versions of cyclooxygenase, with separate functions:

COX-1. This form of the enzyme produces prostaglandins that have beneficial effects, including helping to maintain kidney blood flow, protecting your stomach against harmful acid that can erode its lining and helping blood platelets to function normally in clotting blood.

COX-2. This form of the enzyme is thought to contribute to the development of prostaglandins associated with pain and inflammation.

When researchers realized that traditional NSAIDs blocked both versions of the COX enzyme, the quest was on for a more selective pain reliever — one that would block pain, yet not harm your gastrointestinal lining. This research led to the development of COX-2 inhibitors. The first COX-2 inhibitor was approved by the Food and Drug Administration (FDA) in 1999, and others have since received FDA approval. COX-2 inhibitors are available only by prescription.

Medications now on the market include:
- Celecoxib (Celebrex)
- Rofecoxib (Vioxx)
- Valdecoxib (Bextra)

In clinical studies, COX-2 inhibitors were shown to relieve joint pain just as well as traditional NSAIDs and with fewer side effects. Mainly, the drugs caused fewer ulcers and less gastrointestinal bleeding. Side effects of COX-2 inhibitors are generally mild and may include respiratory infection or inflammation, headache or dizziness. Additional generally mild side effects may include fluid retention, high blood pressure, diarrhea, nausea, heartburn or stomach pain.

Serious but rare side effects include stomach or intestinal bleeding, kidney or liver problems and allergic reactions. Because the medications have been available for a limited time, possible long-term effects of COX-2 inhibitors aren't yet known.

The most effective use of COX-2 inhibitors in the treatment of arthritis is still emerging. But if you have arthritic pain and have experienced gastrointestinal problems from traditional NSAIDs — or are at high risk of such problems — a COX-2 inhibitor may be a good alternative.

COX-2 inhibitors don't have aspirin's antiplatelet effect. It's still uncertain whether taking COX-2 inhibitors affects your risk of stroke or heart attack. Certainly, if you take an aspirin daily to prevent blood clotting, you'll need to continue doing so despite use of a COX-2 inhibitor.

Corticosteroids

A main goal in treating rheumatoid arthritis is to stop inflammation because inflammation can cause permanent damage to the affected areas, as well as pain and discomfort.

Corticosteroids (also called steroids, or glucocorticoids) are the second of the two major types of drugs used to fight inflammation in people with rheumatoid arthritis. Corticosteroids work by impeding your body's ability to make substances that can cause inflammation, such as prostaglandins.

Corticosteroids also serve another function for people with rheumatoid arthritis. Evidence suggests that rheumatoid arthritis may be an autoimmune disease. This means that your immune system mistakenly attacks healthy tissue instead of attacking "invaders" such as bacteria and viruses. Corticosteroids lower autoimmune activity, thus lowering its potential to do harm. For example, they cause white blood cells to work less effectively. Unfortunately, this means that, at the same time, the ability of the body's immune system to fend off infection is reduced to varying degrees in different people.

Corticosteroids are drugs, but they're also hormones that are derived from a hormone called cortisol. Cortisol is produced by your adrenal glands. It has many vital functions in your body. It helps regulate the balance of water and salt and your body's use (metabolism) of protein, fat and carbohydrates. During times of stress — such as an illness or a period of emotional upset — your adrenal glands excrete extra cortisol to help your body deal with the stress.

Although the names resemble each other, corticosteroids aren't the same as the anabolic steroids used by athletes to enhance their performance in competition. Anabolic steroids have no value in treating arthritis. In fact, *steroid* refers to several related chemical substances, including many hormones, bile acids, natural drugs such as digitalis compounds, and the beginning forms (precursors) of some vitamins.

Corticosteroids became widely known more than a half-century ago, when scientists led by physicians and investigators at Mayo Clinic discov-

---

Half-life

Applied to a medication that you're taking, the term *half-life* describes the time that the drug remains effective — doing what it's supposed to do. Technically speaking, that means about the length of time it takes for one-half of a dose of medication to be eliminated from your body. You could also say that it's the recommended time between taking doses.

Some medications have very short half-lives. For 2 plain aspirin or 2 ibuprofen tablets, the half-life is about 4 hours. But some nonsteroidal anti-inflammatory drugs, such as piroxicam (Feldene), have a half-life of about 24 hours. Gold (a disease-modifying antirheumatic drug) injected into the muscle can have a half-life of 3 or 4 months.

---

ered them and began using them to treat arthritis with remarkably positive results. At the time, it was thought that a cure was at hand for arthritis. However, in succeeding years it became clear that because of their toxicity, corticosteroids couldn't be used in high doses for long periods. The side effects were sometimes worse than the symptoms of the arthritis.

When corticosteroids are needed

If you have rheumatoid arthritis, your doctor may first turn to NSAIDs in an attempt to control the inflammation and provide you with some relief. With the different NSAIDs available, several alternatives may be tried if the first choice doesn't work. But the NSAIDs you try may not be potent enough to reduce the inflammation, or they may cause side effects that create additional problems for you.

That's when corticosteroids come into the fight against inflammation. For many people, corticosteroids are likely to be needed only occasionally. However, for others, a low dose of corticosteroid may be needed for long periods of time. In both osteoarthritis and rheumatoid arthritis, cortisone can be injected into the joint and have good results when only one or a few joints are severely affected. When the rheumatoid arthritis is severe and more than one joint is affected, a corticosteroid, often prednisone, can be taken by mouth.

Given the serious side effects, use of corticosteroids in the treatment of arthritis depends very much on their effective and safe management. In other words, your doctor needs to devise a treatment plan that not only works but also keeps these side effects to an absolute minimum. And you must take these drugs *exactly* as your physician instructs you. They are, after all, even more powerful drugs than NSAIDs.

Nevertheless, corticosteroids are adaptable to the varying needs of people with rheumatoid arthritis and other inflammatory diseases. They can be used in several ways:

- Short-term or long-term
- Small doses or large doses
- Taken by mouth or injection

Short-term therapy

Some people with rheumatoid arthritis need quick relief of their symptoms. For instance, they may have a flare-up of the disease that is painful, incapacitating or potentially damaging. If this happens to you, your doctor may put you on a short course of corticosteroids (steroid taper), which commonly produces relief in a matter of a few days. It may also be used to tide you over — allowing you to feel better and reduce damage while you wait for other medications to become effective.

With a short course of corticosteroids, you begin with a moderate dose of the corticosteroid that your doctor prescribes. Then every few days after that you take a smaller and smaller dose of the drug. This approach minimizes the possibility of side effects. To simplify matters for you, special packages of corticosteroids are available that follow the doses of the steroid taper exactly. You need only take the pills indicated, day by day, throughout the specified period. This drug therapy may last a week or two. Because of the significant amounts of corticosteroids used in steroid tapers, they shouldn't be used very often. Intramuscular injections of a corticosteroid can also be used as a short-term approach to treating rheumatoid arthritis.

When other methods such as NSAIDs, lifestyle approaches, disease-modifying antirheumatic drugs or even low doses of oral corticosteroids fail to help, injection of corticosteroids in one or more joints is another option. This can dramatically reduce inflammation in one or several affected areas of your body, such as a knee or an elbow.

Relief may last for months, allowing a break in the cycle of inflammation and injury. This result can mean that injections may be helpful in the future. If there's no significant relief — if it lasts only briefly — then injections aren't for you.

People with osteoarthritis and accompanying inflammation also may be helped by corticosteroid injections. Corticosteroids in pill form are not considered appropriate for osteoarthritis. Corticosteroid injections may be helpful in acute or chronic tendinitis or bursitis.

Although corticosteroid injections — like steroid tapers — generally don't have serious side effects, they mustn't be overused. In fact, numerous injections in the same area of your body may cause damage to the tissues they come into contact with.

Long-term therapy

Using a corticosteroid, such as prednisone, during a long period at doses of more than 10 milligrams (mg) daily almost inevitably produces significant side effects. But low-dose corticosteroids often must be taken by people with severe, unremitting rheumatoid arthritis for years at a time to keep the disease controlled. The possibility of side effects is much less with low doses, but side effects always occur to some extent.

A low-dose course of corticosteroids may be used together with a disease-modifying antirheumatic drug (DMARD), providing you with relief until the DMARD begins to take effect. That could be a period of months. If the DMARD does help you, the dose of the corticosteroids can eventually be tapered and then use of the drug discontinued completely. Alternatively, your doctor may prescribe a low-dose corticosteroid and DMARD together for an indefinite period, especially if the DMARD doesn't work as hoped.

For long-term use of corticosteroids, your doctor will prescribe a daily dose of about 5 to 10 mg of prednisone, or an equivalent dose of a similar drug. Another approach when you're receiving long-term therapy is to alternate the dose you take every few days. You may have a higher dose on day one and a lower dose (or no dose at all) on day two. The anti-inflammatory effect of the drug may not be as effective on the day the lower dose is taken. But if the effect does persist, your body gets the benefit of a low- or no-dose day. Tapering from use of a low dose may take months or years.

Even at small doses, it's vital that you explicitly follow your doctor's directions for taking your corticosteroids. Any improvised changes you make in the way you take your medication — because you think it might make you feel better — can lead to serious side effects.

Corticosteroids by name

There are several different types of corticosteroids. Your physician will select the type that's most appropriate for you. Some leading corticosteroids include the following:

- Cortisone (Cortone Acetate)
- Methylprednisolone (Medrol)
- Prednisolone (Prelone)
- Prednisone (Deltasone, Orasone)
- Triamcinolone (Aristocort)

Corticosteroids are available in both brand names and less costly generic forms. They come as capsules and tablets, liquids for injection, as topical creams and in syrup form for children.

Corticosteroid side effects

When doses of corticosteroids are small — 7.5 mg or less of prednisone or the equivalent of other corticosteroids — the risk of side effects is reduced. Intermediate doses of 7.5 to 20 mg a day for a month are associated with a modest risk. High doses of 20 to 60 mg involve a higher risk and should be taken only when absolutely required. Very high doses — 100 to 1,000 mg a day — are used very rarely and only very briefly.

Corticosteroids have many side effects, ranging from those that are very common to others that are relatively rare. Some very common side effects include the following:

- Weight gain from water retention
- Weight gain from increase in body fat partly due to increased appetite
- Mood swings
- Nervousness
- Sleeplessness
- Easy bruising
- Slow healing of wounds
- Acne
- The development of a round face
- Blurred vision
- Arm- or leg-muscle weakness
- Thinning hair or excessive hair growth
- Osteoporosis

Side effects that are likeliest to happen in people who use moderate or high doses of corticosteroids include the following:

- Increased blood sugar level
- High blood pressure
- Stomach ulcers or irritation, usually when NSAIDs also are being taken
- Purple or red stretch marks on the skin
- Increased risk of infections

Drug interactions

People often use various medications prescribed to them by different physicians — specialists as well as their primary care doctors. They may also use OTC drugs. Unfortunately, the action of one drug can be altered by the action of another, either negating the desired effect or producing a dangerous reaction. Even OTC drugs can cause serious interactions with prescription drugs.

Thus, as you take medications for your arthritis, you must notify your doctor about every medication you use, even nonprescription medications. Bring all of your current medications whenever you visit any physician. That way, proper dosages can be figured for both prescription and nonprescription drugs. And, if needed, a medicine calendar can be arranged for you. You can take the drugs you need to take, but minimize the chances of any interactions.

Some people are more susceptible to the risks of even small doses of corticosteroids than are others. Older adults are more apt to have trouble than younger people.

In one sense, corticosteroids also can be thought of as causing dependency. If you're taking high doses, a dependency on the drug can develop because the high doses can cause your adrenal glands to stop making cortisol. If you've been taking corticosteroids for a long time, your body can't make enough cortisol. This can lead to an adrenal crisis — a potentially fatal development. Some situations in which that may occur include the following:

- During a heart attack
- After an operation
- During an illness
- While you're unconscious and unable to communicate that you're taking corticosteroids

If you're using corticosteroids for a long period, it may be a good idea to wear a medical alert bracelet or necklace or other medical identification. Then, if you're unable to communicate during an adrenal crisis, the medical personnel helping will know they need to give you an extra dose.

Drug interactions are also possible with corticosteroids. That's why it's important to inform your doctor of any other medications that you may be using.

Take, for example, the widely used generic corticosteroid prednisone. If you have diabetes and are taking insulin, you may need to take an increased dose while you're taking prednisone. Although rare, taking the immunosuppressant drug cyclosporine while taking prednisone may increase the chance of convulsions. Prednisone can change the effects of other drugs you're taking, or have its effects changed. Some of those other drugs include the following:

- Amphotericin B
- Estrogen drugs
- Oral contraceptives
- Phenobarbital
- Strong diuretics, such as Lasix
- Blood thinners, such as Coumadin

DMARDs

Anti-inflammatory medications such as NSAIDs are valuable for their ability to repress the inflammation that can damage your joints if you have rheumatoid arthritis. But they do little to affect the basic disease process. For that sort of effect, doctors often turn to a class of medications called disease-modifying antirheumatic drugs (DMARDs). They're also sometimes called remittive or slow-acting drugs.

DMARDs (DE-mards) have been used for years, primarily as second-line drugs against rheumatoid arthritis. These slow-acting drugs have tended to be given to patients for whom a less powerful medication alone — an NSAID, for instance — didn't do the job. They are also useful in limiting the amount of corticosteroid needed to control the disease, thus reducing the risk of side effects from these drugs.

Lately, however, doctors have begun to prescribe DMARDs at early stages in the development of rheumatoid arthritis. As an early line of defense, aggressive use of DMARDs may help slow the disease and save the joints and other tissue from permanent damage. Because they usually act slowly (you may take a DMARD for months before you notice any benefit), they're typically used with an NSAID or a corticosteroid. While the NSAID or corticosteroid handles your immediate symptoms and limits current inflammation, the DMARD goes to work on the disease itself. It also has some effect in limiting inflammation and damage to joints.

Another development in the use of DMARDs is to prescribe them in combination. Studies have shown that people who respond well to one

DMARD — even only to a degree — may benefit further with the addition of another DMARD. Sometimes three DMARDs may be combined.

DMARDs seem to do their job by having some effect on immune systems that have gone out of control. However, it's unclear exactly how these drugs manage to tame immune systems.

There are several different DMARDs that your doctor may consider prescribing for you. Several of the most commonly used are listed here:

- Hydroxychloroquine (Plaquenil)
- Gold (Myochrysine, Solganal)
- Sulfasalazine (Azulfidine)
- Minocycline (Minocin)
- Biologic agents (etanercept, infliximab, anakinra)

Hydroxychloroquine

Among DMARDs, hydroxychloroquine (Plaquenil) has a reputation for having relatively few side effects. Originally a treatment for malaria, the medication has been on the market for many years. Apart from hydroxychloroquine's seeming ability to affect the way immune cells work, scientists don't completely understand how it helps tame the disease process.

Hydroxychloroquine has to be taken daily in a dose of one or two tablets. In fact, you may be able to take a two-tablet dose at the same time. The medication needs about 6 weeks to begin working and 12 to 24 weeks to provide its full benefit. Its relative lack of side effects relieves you of the need for frequent blood tests and doctor's visits.

The drug's uncommon side effects are an upset stomach and rash. A rare effect is muscular weakness. A major side effect — which also occurs rarely — is damage to the eyes. Exposure to bright sunlight may increase the odds of this side effect occurring. So if you're using hydroxychloroquine, you may want to take the precaution of wearing sunglasses and a broad-brimmed hat when you're outside on a sunny day. In any event, have your eyes checked by an ophthalmologist every 6 to 12 months after using the medication for a year. Hydroxychloroquine is often given for a year or more. If a DMARD is not adequately effective itself, another one may be prescribed for an added benefit.

Gold

Gold (Myochrysine, Solganal) is a powerful pharmaceutical treatment that requires regular supervision from your physician. It's capable of producing certain dangerous side effects. Gold — actually, a gold salt and not the metal gold used in jewelry — is generally not used for treating any ailments other than rheumatoid arthritis. A significant percentage (about 60 percent) of people who take gold early in the development of their arthritis have good results.

At the outset of a possible course of gold therapy, your doctor will begin by giving you a test dose of the drug. If you don't have a bad reaction to this, you'll usually start on weekly gold therapy. The dose is small at the outset, then gradually is increased to a full dose. You'll continue to get that full dose once a week for about 5 months. Your physician then makes adjustments, according to your needs. Perhaps you'll be able to go a month without the medication.

Gold is administered two ways. You can take it as an injection in your buttock or as a capsule. You and your doctor will decide which is the best method for you.

The belief that an injection is more likely to produce positive results is partly balanced with the inconvenience of visiting the doctor's office and the discomfort of the procedure. Moreover, your blood and urine must be tested at the same time.

Gold in capsule form, such as auranofin (Ridaura), is given in a daily dose of one or two capsules. In addition to avoiding the discomfort of a weekly injection, this form of gold also requires less frequent monitoring of blood and urine — perhaps just once a month. As with any potent prescription drug, your dosage should never be altered unless your doctor has given the go-ahead.

Gold therapy is associated with these three major side effects:
• Kidney damage
• Damage to bone marrow
• Rashes

Side effects can be extremely serious and are the reasons you need to have your blood and urine tested at regular intervals. Fortunately, they are often mild and disappear when gold therapy is discontinued. Oral gold also may produce diarrhea. Gold preparations aren't used as often as they once were.

Sulfasalazine

Sulfasalazine (Azulfidine) is similar to hydroxychloroquine in its effectiveness.

Although originally developed as a treatment for rheumatoid arthritis, this medication is perhaps best known as an effective treatment of inflammatory bowel disease. Its ability to reduce inflammation seems to be due, in part, to an antibiotic effect it has on bacteria in the bowel. Several years ago, doctors began to notice an improvement in arthritic symptoms in people with rheumatoid arthritis who were taking the medication for bowel disease. This finding confirmed earlier reports from Sweden. Now the drug is widely used to treat both conditions.

If your doctor prescribes sulfasalazine, you'll probably begin with two or three 500-mg doses daily, increasing to as many as six 500-mg tablets a day if necessary and if you don't experience troublesome side effects.

Don't expect immediate relief. The potential benefits may not be noticeable for more than 3 months.

Your doctor will order periodic blood tests to monitor the effect of the medication on your blood cells. Changes are rare. Some people have stomach discomfort, which usually is eliminated by reducing the dose or by taking delayed-action (enteric-coated) tablets.

If you're allergic to sulfa, don't take sulfasalazine. It's a sulfa derivative and could cause an allergic reaction, such as a rash, asthma (wheezing), itching, fever or jaundice.

Side effects and allergies

The term *side effect* simply means a result of taking a medication (or receiving some other medical treatment) that is in addition to the primary and desired effect. Generally, that means some unwanted effect, possibly dangerous.

Many medications used for rheumatoid arthritis have a high potential for serious side effects. These drugs include corticosteroids, NSAIDs, DMARDs and immunosuppressants.

Among possible side effects are drug allergies. Not to be mistaken for an adverse drug reaction, drug allergies are a defective response by your immune system to a medication, just as you might have an allergic reaction to peanuts or plant pollen. Drug allergies manifest in reactions that can be mild (a rash or hives), extremely serious (such as an anaphylactic reaction) or somewhere in between.

Our discussion of side effects in this book is limited to the more important side effects and isn't intended to be complete. Your doctor can provide additional information on effects and side effects of the medications you're taking.

Minocycline

Minocycline (Minocin) is an antibiotic medication that can reduce swelling, tenderness and pain in some cases, but as with other DMARDs it's slow-acting, taking weeks or even months to work. It both has an antibacterial action and works to tame the action of enzymes (metallo-proteinases) that seem to contribute to inflammation in arthritic joints. Your doctor probably will prescribe 100-mg doses to be taken twice daily.

Minocycline is often poorly tolerated and has limited effectiveness. It may cause liver damage, as well as nausea, dizziness and a grayish skin discoloration. As with any antibiotic, this medication may lead to an overgrowth of germs that aren't affected by the drug. You might experience diarrhea, yeast infections or you may have stomach distress.

Penicillamine

Penicillamine (Cuprimine, Depen) is used much less than it once was. It can reduce inflammation, but you have to have patience. Its full effect may require many months to develop.

Your doctor may begin with a 250-mg daily dose. After a month on this program, the dose is gradually increased over several months to a maximum of 1,000 mg a day, depending on your needs and ability to deal with potential side effects.

The side effects of penicillamine are similar to those of gold shots, but they may be more severe, including rash, kidney problems, anemia and muscle weakness. Your doctor may check you for side effects every 2 to 4 weeks.

Immunosuppressants

Because rheumatoid arthritis is an autoimmune disease, it makes sense to look at medications that somehow are able to manage immune systems that are out of control. That's just what immunosuppressant drugs do — though the exact means aren't fully understood. In addition, some of these drugs are cytotoxic, which means they attack and eliminate cells that are associated with the disease. These drugs are usually considered to be DMARDs.

Several major types of immunosuppressant drugs are used by people with rheumatoid arthritis. The generic and brand names of the most commonly used include the following:

- Azathioprine (Imuran)
- Cyclophosphamide (Cytoxan)

- Cyclosporine (Neoral, Sandimmune)
- Leflunomide (Arava)
- Methotrexate (Rheumatrex)

Although sometimes considered a DMARD, methotrexate is more often listed as an immunosuppressant medication.

Like most DMARDs, immunosuppressants can have major and potentially dangerous side effects. They may be best reserved for people with severe problems associated with their rheumatoid arthritis. These medications may cause anemia and an increased likelihood of infection by reducing your body's ability to produce blood cells and suppressing the cells active in fighting infection. Some seem to increase the likelihood of developing certain types of cancer after extensive use. Many can cause liver and kidney problems, and all, especially methotrexate, cyclophosphamide and leflunomide, should be avoided by women who want to become pregnant.

Methotrexate

Methotrexate (Rheumatrex) is an antimetabolite drug. That means it does its job by blocking cells that are responsible for some of the pain, inflammation and damage caused by rheumatoid arthritis. In effect, it dampens the immune system, cutting down on inflammation. It also may slow the growth of synovial membrane cells lining the joint.

Methotrexate has been available for decades as a therapy for psoriasis and cancer. Because of its generally good risk-to-benefit profile and its relatively low cost, methotrexate is the most commonly used DMARD in the United States. Methotrexate is often combined with a DMARD or other immunosuppressant. This is a powerful medication and must be used exactly as your doctor instructs.

Methotrexate is taken by mouth as tablets or liquid and by injection. The liquid form is generally equally beneficial as the tablet form and is cheaper. Some doctors ask that methotrexate be taken in three doses every 12 hours once a week. Others may prescribe it to be taken in a single dose once a week.

It may not be appropriate for you to take methotrexate if:
- You're pregnant or plan to become pregnant
- You're breast-feeding
- You have medical problems such as kidney, liver or lung disease
- You're allergic to methotrexate
- You're taking any kind of prescription or OTC medications or supplements

Genes may hold key to drug reactions

Many people with rheumatoid arthritis have had successful results from treatment with immunosuppressant drugs such as azathioprine. In a small number, however, azathioprine produces life-threatening toxic reactions. Doctors at Mayo Clinic have discovered a gene, thiopurine methyltransferase (TPMT), that may help predict which people are most at risk of these kinds of reactions.

Researchers found that the TPMT genes in some people have mutations that appear to cause no problems by themselves. However, people with these mutant genes experience severe reactions to azathioprine. By testing patients for this mutation, doctors know when this drug can be safely prescribed.

- You're routinely exposed to people with colds and other infections
- You've been treated with X-rays or cancer drugs
- You use alcohol

Side effects may vary from individual to individual. Some of them are:

- Nausea or stomach pain
- Diarrhea
- Loss of appetite
- Loss of hair
- Mouth ulcers or sores
- Rashes
- Inflammation of the lung
- Liver failure
- Anemia

Cytotoxic drugs such as methotrexate can also inhibit the infection-fighting potency of your white blood cells, lower the number of platelets (which makes you bruise or bleed more easily) and cut down on your red blood cells (causing fatigue). Whenever you notice these or any other possible side effects, contact your doctor.

If your doctor prescribes methotrexate, you'll need to have your blood tested regularly. This testing helps ensure that the drug doesn't produce any unwanted changes in your liver and bone marrow. Blood tests and visits with your doctor can help deal with any developing side effects in a timely manner.

Azathioprine

Azathioprine (Imuran) is a drug that has been used most commonly to help the body accept kidney and heart transplants that might otherwise be attacked by the immune system and rejected. It holds the white blood cells in check, helping to restrain the autoimmune effects that are part of rheumatoid arthritis. Of course, that also means that your body's ability to fight off infection is weakened.

Some of the drug's other notable side effects include the following:
- Gastrointestinal distress, such as heartburn, nausea and vomiting
- Bleeding and bruising more easily than normal
- Fatigue
- Loss of appetite
- Fevers and chills

Once again, your doctor will supervise your progress while you're taking azathioprine, including blood tests every few weeks. You might take the medication for a long time. Your dosage is based on your body weight, and you take the medication with food.

It's particularly important that you avoid taking azathioprine at the same time you take a gout drug called allopurinol. Their combination in your body adds to the toxic effect and, if used, requires special dosing and close supervision.

Drug absorption

The absorption of a medication into your system can be modified in different ways.

Taking a drug with food or an antacid can slow or prevent the absorption of a drug, while protecting your stomach from its potentially harsh effects. In fact, some arthritis medications — such as corticosteroids — are prescribed to be taken with food. NSAIDs should be taken with food, liquid or an antacid. Yet others, such as some DMARDs and minocycline, are prescribed to be taken on an empty stomach.

The absorption of a medication can also be delayed by taking tablets that have something called an enteric coating. This coating prevents absorption until the medication has arrived in the small intestine, preventing potential stomach irritation or other problems.

Cyclosporine

For the most part, cyclosporine (Neoral) has been used as a drug for people who have had organ transplants. It benefits them by helping to prevent the immune system from rejecting the newly transplanted organ. The drug does its job by suppressing some of the cells that play a role in the inflammation associated with rheumatoid arthritis. It's usually kept in reserve for patients who don't respond to the more widely used DMARDs, such as methotrexate, hydroxychloroquine and others.

Your dosage — between 200 mg and 400 mg a day in one dose or two — is determined by your weight. It's important that you take the medication at the same time each day. It doesn't matter if you take it with or without food. The dose is often monitored by its level in the blood.

Although cyclosporine doesn't cause problems with the bone marrow — unlike other immunosuppressants and DMARDs such as gold — it does come with side effects. It can cause the following:

• Kidney damage
• Muscle tremors
• High blood pressure
• Excessive hair growth
• Excessive growth of the gums

Because of cyclosporine's potential for causing kidney damage, you must have your blood tested. How often you need testing depends on factors such as your response to the medication and whether you have pre-existing heart or kidney problems.

There are several factors that may make the use of cyclosporine more questionable:

• A sensitivity to castor oil, if you are taking the drug by injection
• Any kidney or liver disease
• Hypertension
• A current infection

Cyclophosphamide

Your doctor will turn to cyclophosphamide (Cytoxan) only in very serious situations, such as if your rheumatoid arthritis extends to other tissues, especially if it inflames your blood vessels.

This extremely potent medication kills cells by damaging their genetic information. In particular, it kills lymphocytes that are part of an autoimmune disease. Unfortunately, the drug can't tell the difference between cells that are part of the disease process and cells that are performing normal functions.

Side effects include:

- Low blood cell counts
- Increased infections
- Bleeding in the bladder
- Bladder cancer and other cancers
- Hair loss
- Increased risk of certain cancers, if taken for a long period

Given cyclophosphamide's potential for producing serious side effects, your doctor will want to monitor you very closely while you're taking the drug. You'll have to have blood tests at regular intervals — every 2 or 3 weeks. You should notify your physician if you have any problems with bleeding, bruising or fatigue.

You'll take this medication in tablet form with your breakfast. And when you're using the drug, be sure to drink plenty of fluids. Take care to urinate before going to bed. These steps can help protect your bladder from possible damage.

If you have an active infection or liver or kidney disease, notify your doctor. These ailments may affect your ability to take this medication.

Leflunomide

Leflunomide (Arava) is an immunosuppressant shown to reduce pain, stiffness, inflammation and swelling. It also may slow or halt joint damage associated with rheumatoid arthritis. People taking the medication generally notice an improvement in symptoms within 1 to 3 months.

Similar to other immunosuppressants, the drug inhibits certain substances — in this case a type of enzyme — produced by your immune system. Leflunomide may cause a range of side effects, including abdominal pain, back pain, bronchitis, cough, diarrhea, headache and indigestion. Serious side effects may include liver damage and a reduced ability to fight off infection. Your doctor will test your liver function before you begin taking the medication and will conduct monthly tests thereafter. If you have a liver condition, you may not be able to take the medication. If you develop liver problems while taking the drug, your dose will have to be reduced or stopped.

Leflunomide also shouldn't be taken if you're pregnant, breastfeeding or contemplating pregnancy. It can harm the developing fetus and may cause serious side effects in nursing infants. Because of the medication's long half-life, it can take many months to completely eliminate it from your system. If needed, elimination of the drug can be sped up by using cholestyramine, prescribed by your doctor.

Biologic agents

For a number of years, scientists have been studying certain proteins called cytokines (SI-to-kines) that contribute to arthritis. Cytokines are substances made by certain cells that influence other cells and eventually lead to inflammation and joint degeneration.

Biologic agents are medications that interfere with the development or action of cytokines. The drugs are intended to go beyond symptom relief to actually stop joint damage and inflammation.

Three biologic agents to receive FDA approval are:
• Anakinra (Kineret)
• Etanercept (Enbrel)
• Infliximab (Remicade)

There are two groups of biologic agents available for treating rheumatoid arthritis. Etanercept and infliximab work by blocking a specific cytokine called tumor necrosis factor-alpha (TNF-alpha). The other, anakinra, works by blocking a cytokine called interleukin-1 (IL-1).

Etanercept

Etanercept (Enbrel) is used to treat symptoms of moderate to severe rheumatoid arthritis. The drug mimics the action of TNF-alpha receptors naturally found in your body, "soaking up" excess TNF-alpha, which helps to reduce inflammation.

Unlike other immunosuppressant medications that affect a larger part of your immune system, etanercept targets a smaller, specific component of the disease process.

Etanercept has been shown to provide significant symptom relief. The drug can be taken along with other medications commonly used to treat rheumatoid arthritis, including methotrexate, corticosteroids and pain relievers.

Etanercept is generally prescribed when traditional medications have proved inadequate because the drug is more costly and more complicated to take than some other medications. Etanercept is given by injection twice a week under the skin of your thigh, abdomen or upper arm. You can inject the medication yourself at home or receive the injections at your doctor's office.

Filtering out harmful substances

A unique method for treating rheumatoid arthritis involves a blood-filtering device. Called a selective extracorporeal immunoadsorption column (Prosorba column), the technique works somewhat like kidney dialysis.

Blood is drawn from a vein in an arm and then is pumped through a cell separator (apheresis machine). This machine separates the liquid part of your blood (plasma) from blood cells. The plasma then passes through the Prosorba column, a plastic cylinder about the size of a coffee mug. The cylinder contains a sand-like substance coated with a special material called protein A. Protein A is thought to bind to certain substances (immune complexes and antigens) involved in the inflammatory process, removing the substances from your blood. The filtered plasma is reunited with your blood cells and returned to your body through a vein in your other arm. The entire procedure takes about 2 hours.

The number of treatments you receive is based on your condition. One treatment a week for 12 weeks is typically recommended. Not all people respond to the treatment, but in clinical studies, many participants noticed at least some improvement in symptoms. It often takes 1 to 3 months before benefits of the therapy become noticeable.

The most common side effects are flu-like conditions and a short-term flare in joint pain and swelling for a couple of days after treatment. Because the filtering process can lower your blood pressure, you may not be a candidate for this therapy if you have a heart condition or are taking medication for high blood pressure.

Side effects of the medication may include abdominal pain, fever, reduced white blood cell count, dizziness, headache, indigestion, respiratory problems and injection site reactions, such as rash and itching. Although it's not known whether etanercept changes the body's ability to resist infection, people taking the drug should heighten their awareness of exposure to infection, including fungal infections and tuberculosis. Serious, even fatal, infections may occur, especially in people whose immune systems are already weakened. If you're taking medications that can weaken your immune system, you may not be a candidate for etanercept. In addition, because it may worsen congestive heart failure, people with this disorder shouldn't take etanercept.

Infliximab

Infliximab (Remicade) inhibits TNF-alpha by neutralizing its biological activity, reducing the inflammatory process from the start. Infliximab is usually given with methotrexate to enhance effectiveness and reduce side effects.

Like etanercept, infliximab is more costly and complicated to administer and therefore is generally prescribed when other medications haven't been effective. Infliximab is given by intravenous infusion. The process involves inserting a tiny tube (catheter) into your arm. The drug is administered through the catheter during a 2-hour period. Additional doses are given at 2 weeks and 6 weeks. Maintenance doses are then usually administered every 8 weeks.

Side effects of the medication may include respiratory problems, rash, fever, headache, nausea, diarrhea and worsening of congestive heart failure. Like etanercept, infliximab also weakens your immune system response. Because of concern about increased risk of infections such as tuberculosis (TB), or the reactivation of tuberculosis, you should have a negative TB test before beginning treatment with infliximab.

There are reports that some people have developed symptoms of autoimmune disorders while taking infliximab, such as lupus-like or multiple sclerosis-like disease.

If you have another health condition or are taking medications that can weaken your immune system, you may not be a candidate for infliximab.

Analgesic vs. anti-inflammatory

Although sometimes a drug may have both anti-inflammatory and analgesic effects — specifically, aspirin and other NSAIDs — these two functions are different.

Analgesics relieve pain. Narcotic analgesics are available by prescription only and are generally reserved for the relief of severe pain. Many are potentially addictive. Nonnarcotic analgesics, such as acetaminophen and aspirin, are used for mild pain.

Anti-inflammatory drugs (NSAIDs and corticosteroids) used for rheumatoid arthritis reduce the inflammation that can cause permanent damage to joints. Inflammation results in an increased blood flow, which produces swelling, redness, pain and heat.

Anakinra

Anakinra (Kineret) is a new biologic agent for treatment of rheumatoid arthritis. It works by inhibiting the cytokine interleukin-1 (IL-1), a protein that promotes inflammation. The drug blocks the interleukin-1 receptor antagonist (IL-1Ra), which reduces the activity of IL-1.

Anakinra, like etanercept and infliximab, is expensive and used mainly for people who aren't responding to conventional treatment. The daily dose is given by self-administered injection under the skin of your thigh or abdomen. Like other biologic agents, anakinra has been effective in reducing the pain and swelling of rheumatoid arthritis in clinical trials. It also appears to slow the progression of joint damage. Benefits of anakinra may be evident in the first week of treatment, but the maximum results may not be felt for a month or longer.

Side effects of taking anakinra include rash and itching at the injection site, which can be treated with a mild steroid cream. Other infrequent side effects include temporary reduction in white blood cell count, headache and an increase in upper respiratory infections.

Pain reducers (analgesics)

When arthritis causes pain, you naturally want relief as quickly as possible. Analgesics, or painkillers, can provide that relief, but some come with serious side effects, including addiction. As with any other medication, your body eventually develops a tolerance for painkillers, so the longer you take them, the less effective they are. In addition, by masking your pain, these drugs may fool you into thinking that you can do more activity than you should, leading to additional damage or injury.

The two most familiar nonaddictive analgesics are aspirin and acetaminophen. Aspirin, as discussed earlier in this chapter, is also an NSAID and therefore may cause stomach irritation in some people. Acetaminophen (Tylenol, others) is a nonaddictive OTC painkiller that is not an NSAID. It is less likely than aspirin or other NSAIDs to irritate your stomach, but it has only a little effect on inflammation. However, some people with arthritis find that acetaminophen can ease their discomfort as effectively as an NSAID.

If needed, you can use an NSAID with acetaminophen for a short time. But remember that you shouldn't take more than the recommended dose of acetaminophen because it can lead to liver problems, especially in people who consume three or more alcoholic drinks daily.

An analgesic that is neither an NSAID nor a narcotic is tramadol (Ultram). For many people, this analgesic is effective for pain relief. It may cause nausea.

Most other analgesics are narcotics that may become addictive and shouldn't be used routinely to treat arthritis. The strongest of these are derived from opium or are made synthetically to have opium-like characteristics. Unfortunately, people who are most likely to develop an addiction to narcotic analgesics are those who have chronic pain.

Narcotic painkillers include the following:
- Codeine
- Hydrocodone
- Meperidine (Demerol)
- Oxycodone (OxyContin)
- Propoxyphene (Darvon-N)

Topical pain relievers

Topical pain relievers are creams, lotions, gels or sprays that you put on your skin. Available as OTC products, they can help temporarily ease some types of arthritis pain.

Topical pain relievers work in different ways. Some contain irritants such as menthol or oil of wintergreen that produce a distracting sensation (Arthricare Double Ice, Eucalyptamint, Icy Hot). Others contain salicylates, the same ingredients that give aspirin its pain-relieving quality. Products with salicylates (Ben-Gay, Aspercreme, Sportscreme) may actually reduce inflammation in muscles and joints by being absorbed through the skin, in addition to relieving pain.

Capsaicin (Capzasin-P, Zostrix), a cream made from the seeds of hot chili peppers, is most effective for arthritic joints close to your skin surface, such as your fingers, knees and elbows. Capsaicin works by depleting your nerve cells of a chemical called substance P that's important for sending pain messages. You periodically rub the medication on your skin, typically three or four times a day. You may feel an initial burning sensation where the cream is applied. It usually takes about 1 or 2 weeks before you begin to feel significant pain relief.

When using topical pain relievers, be careful not to rub or touch your eyes until you've washed your hands thoroughly. Don't use these pain relievers on broken or irritated skin or in combination with a heating pad or bandage. If you are allergic to aspirin or are taking an anticoagulant blood thinner, check with your doctor before using topical medications that contain salicylates.

Antidepressant drugs

Living with arthritis can produce depression in some people. Studies of people with chronic diseases, including arthritis, have found that about one in five report feelings of depression. People who experience greater pain and disability or have more unpredictable occurrences of pain are understandably more likely to feel discouraged or depressed.

If your arthritis has caused feelings of depression, your doctor may prescribe an antidepressant drug. These prescription drugs can help treat the depression and insomnia that often accompany chronic pain. Because these drugs do cause some side effects and may not work as effectively for some people, your doctor may have you try different drugs until you find one that works best for you.

Tricyclic antidepressants are most often prescribed for people with arthritis. These include the following:
- Amitriptyline (Elavil, Endep)
- Desipramine (Norpramin)
- Imipramine (Tofranil)
- Nortriptyline (Aventyl, Pamelor)

When tricyclic antidepressants prove ineffective, your doctor may prescribe other antidepressants, such as:
- Sertraline (Zoloft)
- Trazodone (Desyrel)

Even if you don't have depression, antidepressants can help relieve pain and improve sleep. Prescribed in low doses and taken at bedtime, they may help you sleep better and experience less pain.

Antidepressants aren't addictive, so you can use them for a long time. Possible side effects include sedation, constipation, difficulty with urination, weight gain, blurred vision or dry mouth. If you're experiencing dry mouth from taking an antidepressant, ask your doctor about using an antidepressant that doesn't have this side effect.

Muscle relaxants

As their name indicates, muscle relaxants such as cyclobenzaprine (Flexeril) or carisoprodol (Soma) relax the muscles and are often used to treat muscle spasms associated with injury of muscles, bones and joints. Muscle relaxants may help people with fibromyalgia. With arthritis, however, they haven't proved useful and, like tranquilizers, should be avoided.

Tranquilizers

Even in low doses, tranquilizers such as diazepam (Valium), alprazolam (Xanax) and chlordiazepoxide (Librium) are addictive when taken over a sufficient amount of time. In addition, these depressant drugs can be extremely dangerous when mixed with alcohol.

Because tranquilizers aren't effective for treating arthritis and may actually *cause* depression, it's best not to take them for arthritis symptoms.

Visco supplementation

Hyaluronic acid, or hyaluronate, is a natural substance found in normal joint fluid. For people with osteoarthritis in one or both knees, injecting a compound containing hyaluronic acid into a diseased knee joint may improve mobility and reduce pain. The medication is sold under the names hyaluronate (Hyalgan) and hylan G-F 20 (Synvisc).

Hyaluronic acid injections may be recommended for people who can't get relief from pain medication, exercise or physical therapy. Hyalgan is administered as a series of five injections over a period of 5 weeks. A local anesthetic is injected first to ease discomfort from the medication, which must be administered with a large-gauge needle. Relief may last up to 6 months. Synvisc is administered similarly to Hyalgan, but is given in three injections. Relief may last 6 months or longer. With either drug, a second course of shots may be given if the first series of shots appears beneficial. A second round may provide longer-lasting effects.

Researchers continue to debate whether hyaluronic acid is more effective than anti-inflammatory drugs for treating osteoarthritis pain.

Arthritis medications guide

NSAIDs

Generic names	Brand names
Aspirin	Bayer,* Bufferin,* Ascriptin*
Naproxen	Naprelan, Naprosyn
Naproxen sodium	Aleve,* Anaprox
Diclofenac	Voltaren, Cataflam
Diclofenac sodium and misoprostol	Arthrotec
Etodolac	Lodine
Fenoprofen	Nalfon
Flurbiprofen	Ansaid
Ibuprofen	Advil,* Motrin IB,* Nuprin*
Indomethacin	Indocin
Ketoprofen	Actron, Orudis KT,* Oruvail
Nabumetone	Relafen
Choline magnesium trisalicylate	Trilisate
Salsalate	Disalcid, Amigisic
Diflunisal	Dolobid
Oxaprozin	Daypro
Piroxicam	Feldene
Sulindac	Clinoril
Tolmetin	Tolectin
Meloxicam	Mobic

Possible side effects: Mild headache, lightheadedness, drowsiness, dizziness, heartburn, stomach irritation, gastric ulcers and bleeding, decreased kidney function, ringing in the ears and fluid retention

Reminders and cautions: Tell your doctor if you are allergic to aspirin or similar medications, have kidney, liver or heart disease, have high blood pressure, peptic ulcers or asthma, or use blood thinners.

*Available without a prescription.

COX-2 inhibitors

Generic names	Brand names
Celecoxib	Celebrex
Rofecoxib	Vioxx
Valdecoxib	Bextra

Possible side effects: Respiratory infection or inflammation, headache, dizziness, diarrhea, nausea, heartburn, stomach pain, high blood pressure, swelling of the legs and feet, back pain, urinary tract infection, allergic reaction, decreased kidney function, gastrointestinal ulceration and bleeding and elevated liver enzymes

Reminders and cautions: Tell your doctor if you are allergic to aspirin or similar medications, have kidney, liver or heart disease, have high blood pressure, peptic ulcers or asthma, or use blood thinners

Corticosteroids ▪▪▪▪▪▪▪▪▪▪▪▪▪▪▪▪▪▪▪▪▪▪▪▪▪

Generic names	Brand names
Cortisone	Cortone Acetate
Methylprednisolone	Medrol
Prednisolone	Prelone
Prednisone	Deltasone, Orasone, Sterapred
Triamcinolone	Aristocort

Possible side effects: Weight gain from water retention or increase in body fat, mood swings, nervousness, insomnia. People taking moderate or high doses may have an increased blood sugar level, high blood pressure, stomach ulcers or irritation (usually when NSAIDs are also being taken) and purple or red stretch marks.
Reminders and cautions: Dependency can develop because the adrenal glands stop making cortisol, resulting in a potentially dangerous condition called adrenal crisis. If you use corticosteroids for a long time, wear a medical alert bracelet or necklace. Drug interactions are possible, so be sure to inform your doctor of other medications you take.

DMARDs ▪▪▪▪▪▪▪▪▪▪▪▪▪▪▪▪▪▪▪▪▪▪▪▪▪

Generic names	Brand names
Hydroxychloroquine	Plaquenil

Possible side effects: Rare side effects include damage to the eyes, upset stomach and muscle weakness.
Reminders and cautions: When using this drug, you may want to wear sunglasses and a broad-brimmed hat in the sun. Have your eyes checked every 6 to 12 months after using the drug for a year.

Gold	Myochrysine, Solganal, Ridaura

Possible side effects: Kidney damage, bone marrow damage, and rashes
Reminders and cautions: Tell your doctor if you have kidney or liver disease, a blood cell abnormality or inflammatory bowel disease or have had a negative reaction to this drug in the past.

Sulfasalazine	Azulfidine

Possible side effects: Nausea, stomach distress, loss of appetite, vomiting, headache, itching or rash, fever, and anemia
Reminders and cautions: Tell your doctor if you have a sensitivity to sulfa drugs or aspirin, have liver, kidney or blood disease, or have bronchial asthma.

Minocycline   Minocin

Possible side effects: Liver damage, nausea, rash, dizziness, headache, vaginal
infections, anemia, appetite loss, diarrhea, and skin discoloration
Reminders and cautions: Consult your doctor before taking this drug with
antacids, blood thinners, preparations with iron, oral contraceptives or
penicillin. If you are pregnant or plan to become pregnant, inform your
doctor before taking this drug.

Immunosuppressants

Generic names	Brand names
Azathioprine	Imuran

Possible side effects: Decreased ability to fight infection, gastrointestinal distress,
easy bleeding and bruising, fatigue, loss of appetite, fevers and chills
Reminders and cautions: Avoid taking this drug if you have liver or kidney
disease. Don't take with the gout drug allopurinol.

Cyclophosphamide   Cytoxan

Possible side effects: Low blood cell counts, increased infections, bleeding in
bladder, hair loss, increased risk of certain cancers if taken for a long period,
and damage to bone marrow, stomach or bowels
Reminders and cautions: If you have an active infection or liver or kidney
disease, your ability to take this medication may be affected.

Cyclosporine   Neoral, Sandimmune

Possible side effects: Kidney damage or failure, muscle tremors, excessive hair
growth, and excessive growth of the gums
Reminders and cautions: Tell your doctor if you are pregnant or plan to become
pregnant or if you have kidney or liver disease, hypertension, an
infection or a sensitivity to castor oil. Interactions can occur with many other
drugs. Avoid having immunizations or vaccinations while taking this drug.

Methotrexate   Rheumatrex

Possible side effects: Nausea or stomach pain, diarrhea, loss of appetite, loss of
hair, mouth ulcers or sores, rashes, easy bruising or bleeding, and fatigue
Reminders and cautions: Tell your doctor if you are pregnant, are breast feeding,
have kidney or liver disease, have allergies to medications, are exposed to
people with infections, have been treated with X-rays or cancer drugs or use
alcohol.

Leflunomide   Arava

Possible side effects: Diarrhea, temporary loss of hair, rash, high blood pressure or liver problems
Reminders and cautions: Not recommended for children, for women who may become pregnant or for men who could potentially father a child shortly after treatment with Arava.

Biologic agents

Generic names	Brand names

Etanercept   Enbrel

Possible side effects: Injection site reactions (rash, itching, hives), abdominal pain, cough, dizziness, headache, indigestion, infection, rash, nausea, respiratory problems, sinus and nasal inflammation, sore throat, chest pain or heart attack, high or low blood pressure, stomach and intestinal bleeding, and lowered white blood cell count
Reminders and cautions: Tell your doctor if you have a weakened immune system or history of recurring infection, you develop an allergic reaction or infection while taking the medication, you are pregnant or breast-feeding, or you plan to become pregnant in the near future.

Infliximab   Remicade

Possible side effects: Infusion site reaction (hives), respiratory problems, headache, fever, diarrhea, indigestion, infection, cough, difficulty breathing and low blood pressure, and lupus-like or multiple sclerosis-like disease
Reminders and cautions: Tell your doctor if you have a weakened immune system or history of recurring infection, you develop an allergic reaction or infection while taking the medication, you are pregnant or breast-feeding, or you plan to become pregnant in the near future. Have a tuberculosis skin test before taking this drug.

Anakinra   Kineret

Possible side effects: Injection site reactions (rash, itching, hives), flu-like symptoms including cough, runny nose, headache and lowered white blood cell count
Reminders and cautions: Tell your doctor if you have a weakened immune system or history of reoccurring infection or asthma, you develop an allergic reaction or infection while taking the medication, you are pregnant or breast-feeding, or you plan to become pregnant in the near future.

Pain reducers (analgesics) ▬▬▬▬▬▬▬▬▬▬▬▬▬▬▬▬

Generic names	Brand names

Meperidine   Demerol

Possible side effects: Constipation, vomiting, nausea, lightheadedness, dizziness, sedation, and sweating
Reminders and cautions: Use of this drug can lead to addiction. Notify your physician if you have severe kidney or liver problems, hypothyroidism, Addison's disease, head injury, irregular heartbeat, or if you have ever had convulsions.

Oxycodone   OxyContin

Possible side effects: Vomiting, nausea, lightheadedness, dizziness, and sedation
Reminders and cautions: Tell your doctor if you have a head injury, stomach problems, kidney, liver or thyroid disease, Addison's disease, an enlarged prostate, or drug or alcohol abuse problems. Don't take this drug with alcohol.

Propoxyphene   Darvon-N

Possible side effects: Vomiting, nausea, lightheadedness, dizziness, drowsiness, and sedation
Reminders and cautions: Tell your doctor if you have ever experienced serious depression or are using antidepressants or tranquilizers, if you have a kidney or liver problem or if you are pregnant or plan to become pregnant.

Tramadol   Ultram

Possible side effects: Upset stomach, nausea, constipation, drowsiness, and occasional dizziness
Reminders and cautions: Tell your doctor of any medications you are taking because this drug can cause seizures, especially in people taking other medications.

Codeine

Possible side effects: Constipation, fecal impaction, and depression
Reminders and cautions: Tell your doctor if you are constipated. Also, be aware that this narcotic can be addictive.

Hydrocodone   Codone

Possible side effects: Lightheadedness, dizziness, sedation, nausea, vomiting
Reminders and cautions: Tell your doctor if you are constipated. Also, be aware that this narcotic can be addictive.

Medications for arthritis are continually being developed and marketed. For the latest information on medications for arthritis, consult the Mayo Clinic Health Information Web site at *www.MayoClinic.com.*

Mayo Clinic doesn't endorse any company or product. The listing in this Arthritis Medications Guide is incomplete and doesn't include all available medications, side effects from use of the drugs or precautions for using these drugs. Other medication options may be available.

This information supplements the advice of your personal physician, whom you should consult for personal health problems.

Chapter 8

Surgical treatments

I f joint pain is keeping you on the sidelines, a surgical procedure may be one way to a more active, satisfying life. Your doctor may recommend some form of joint operation when other treatments such as medications, physical therapy and weight loss fail to relieve your arthritis symptoms. Surgeons use various procedures to relieve pain, slow or prevent cartilage damage, and restore mobility and stability.

Because joint operations pose some risks, you and your doctor should discuss these issues before deciding whether it's the best option for you. The strength of your bones and the ligaments supporting your joints, your age, your weight and your ability to participate in rehabilitation can all affect the outcome of joint operation. It's also important to understand and accept the limits that it may impose.

Selecting a surgeon

Your personal physician can help you obtain consultation with a surgeon. He or she will usually recommend an orthopedic surgeon who has extensive experience in joint procedures. Orthopedic surgeons perform operations involving joints, muscles and bones.

Board-certified orthopedic surgeons have met training and experience requirements beyond those required for licensure. Some orthopedic surgeons complete additional training and focus their practice on the treatment of specific joints.

It's important to have confidence in the surgeon you choose. An experienced surgeon should be able to answer your questions about how the procedure is performed, the risks and benefits associated with it and what to expect during your recovery.

Given the potential risks and costs associated with surgery, seeking a second opinion before proceeding with an operation may be a sensible option. Either you or your primary physician can initiate the process to get a second opinion. Don't be afraid to bring it up.

Common forms of joint surgery

Many types of surgical procedures are used to treat joints affected by arthritis. Depending on your age and overall health, the form of arthritis you have and your specific joint problems, your surgeon may recommend one or more of the following procedures.

Arthroscopic debridement

Surgeons use this procedure to remove loose fragments of bone, cartilage or synovium that cause joint pain, most often in the knees. During this procedure, the surgeon makes a small incision and inserts an arthroscope. This device is a thin tube through which the surgeon views and suctions out the tissue fragments. In some cases the surgeon may need to insert other surgical instruments through additional small incisions. This procedure is often helpful to people with osteoarthritis.

Synovectomy

The purpose of this procedure is to remove some of the inflamed synovial tissue that lines joints affected by inflammatory arthritis, especially rheumatoid arthritis. Removing this tissue can reduce pain and swelling and delay or possibly prevent the destruction of the cartilage and bone. Although it can provide pain relief, synovectomy is not a cure. The inflammation may recur as the synovium regrows after the operation.

Synovectomy is routinely performed on the fingers, wrists and knees, before significant cartilage erosion or deformity occurs.

Osteotomy

During this procedure, surgeons cut and reposition bones near a damaged joint to help correct deformities caused by arthritis. These adjustments also help slow cartilage damage by distributing your body weight more evenly across the joint. Osteotomy is sometimes used to correct curvature or bowing in the lower leg bones caused by osteoarthritis.

Resection

Surgeons sometimes remove all or part of a damaged bone when diseased joints make movement painful. Resection is frequently used in the feet to make walking easier and in the wrists and hands to reduce pain.

Joint replacement (arthroplasty)

When osteoarthritis or rheumatoid arthritis severely damages a joint, your doctor may recommend a surgical procedure called arthroplasty (AHR-thro-plas-tee). *Arthroplasty* literally means "re-forming of the joint." The operation may involve smoothing the ends of bones in a joint.

In replacement arthroplasty, also called total joint replacement, surgeons remove certain parts of the damaged joint and replace them with a high-density plastic or metal alloy device called a prosthesis or implant. The hip and the knee are the most commonly replaced joints, but implants can also replace shoulder, finger and other joints.

Joint fusion

Also called arthrodesis (ahr-thro-DE-sis), joint fusion is used most often to reduce pain and improve stability in the spine, wrist, ankle and feet. During this procedure surgeons remove a thin layer of tissue from the ends of two bones and bind them together, often using pins, rods or plates. Fresh bone cells then grow and fuse the two bones permanently. Once healed, the fused joint can bear weight, but it has no flexibility. Because it eliminates joint mobility, joint fusion is typically used when total joint replacement isn't possible.

Tendon and ligament adjustments

Surgeons can repair tendon tears to reduce pain, restore function and, in some cases, prevent tendon rupture. Procedures to tighten or loosen tendons and ligaments are sometimes recommended to decrease pain, increase joint mobility or prepare a joint for total joint replacement. Surgeons also perform procedures to relieve pressure on nerves located near damaged joints.

Anatomy of an artificial joint

Artificial joint implants are made of various metals or a plastic-like material (polyethylene). At large medical centers, physicians sometimes use computers to custom design an implant and plan the operation. Large inventories of artificial joints enable surgeons to select the implant best suited to your needs.

Traditionally, surgeons have secured joint implants to bones with a bone cement (methylmethacrylate). But this cement can crack after several years, causing the implant to loosen. If loosening occurs, you may need additional operations to reattach or replace the implant. To address this problem, researchers are exploring new methods of manufacturing and applying the cement.

In some cases, cementless prostheses may improve the durability of implants. These implants have a porous surface into which the bone grows and attaches itself (bone ingrowth). But cementless implants also can loosen.

Over time, both types of artificial joints create debris caused by friction and wear. The shedding of particles can cause irritation that destroys bone and ultimately contributes to loosening.

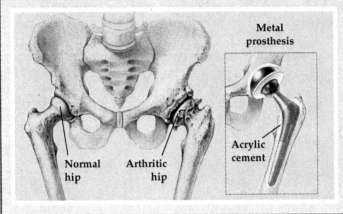

Metal prosthesis

Acrylic cement

Normal hip   Arthritic hip

Gradual deterioration of the hip joint can occur in osteoarthritis. Implanting an artificial hip can help to eliminate pain and restore near-normal function.

Which joints can surgery help?

Because your joints vary in size, shape and design, surgeons must tailor their treatments to accommodate these differences. In this section, we explain how surgeons use the various surgical procedures to relieve arthritis symptoms in specific joints.

Hand and wrist joints

The ability to grasp a spoon, turn a doorknob or open a can of soda is something you may not take for granted if arthritis affects your hands. It's no secret that arthritis pain can make these movements difficult, if not nearly impossible.

Like all joint operations, the goal of procedures on the hands and wrists is to improve function and reduce pain. Although some procedures can improve the appearance of joints deformed by arthritis, surgery is rarely recommended for cosmetic reasons alone.

Sometimes rheumatoid arthritis causes tears in the tendons of the hand and wrist, and an operation is performed to repair the tears and prevent rupture of these tendons. Other surgical procedures help tighten or loosen tendons and ligaments in the hand and wrist to decrease your pain and increase your mobility and grip strength.

Synovectomy may help reduce pain in the wrists and fingers caused by rheumatoid arthritis. Joint fusion can relieve pain and improve stability in severely damaged finger and wrist joints. But wrist fusion causes a decrease in hand mobility.

Hand and wrist joint replacements are performed less often than hip and knee arthroplasties, partly because the joints are small, are close to the skin and require precise repair of ligaments and tendons. Because more conservative procedures such as joint fusion and tendon repairs produce favorable results, many surgeons reserve replacement for only the most severely damaged hand and wrist joints.

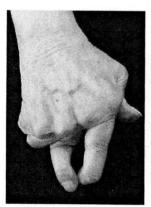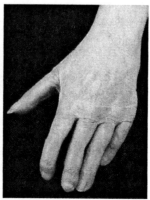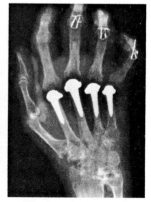

Replacement of diseased or damaged finger joints with artificial ones can provide remarkable improvements in function and appearance. *Left*, The deformed right hand of a person with rheumatoid arthritis. *Center*, The left hand of the same person after joint replacement. *Right*, X-ray of hand with artifical joint implants.

Elbows

Your elbow contains a hinge joint that allows you to bend your arm and rotate your hand to perform various tasks. Even when it's healthy, this complex joint is subject to a great deal of stress.

Synovectomy, performed by itself or with bone resection, can help increase your elbow's range of motion and relieve pain caused by rheumatoid arthritis.

Total joint replacement of the elbow is a relatively new procedure and is generally performed only when joint damage caused by arthritis severely limits the use of the hands and arms. People with severe degenerative arthritis also may be good candidates for this procedure.

Elbow implants are typically secured with a combination of cement and bone growth into the implant (bone ingrowth). Mechanical problems in the artificial joint, such as loosening of the implant or breakage, are more likely to occur in the elbow than in other joints because of the tremendous stress that the elbow undergoes.

Although replacing the elbow joint relieves pain, the return of normal mobility and function is less predictable. Despite this limitation, the procedure usually provides adequate range of motion for most activities of daily living.

Shoulders

Surgeons use various procedures to relieve shoulder pain that doesn't respond to conservative measures. Synovectomy can provide temporary relief for joints inflamed by rheumatoid arthritis. Joint fusion also can reduce pain and offer long-term stability in joints that are more severely damaged. Even though fusion limits flexibility, some motion is still possible after this procedure.

Because the shoulder makes so many intricate motions in various directions, replacing this joint is complex. Surgeons must first repair damaged tendons or ligaments to ensure the implant's stability and function.

As with other joint replacements, the types of shoulder implants used and the methods for securing them vary. Cementless joints exist, but most surgeons have more experience with traditional cemented joints.

When performed by an experienced surgeon, total shoulder arthroplasty restores almost two-thirds of normal shoulder motion. However, a longer rehabilitation period is necessary with shoulder replacement than with other types of joint replacements. Strengthening and stretching exercises help ensure a return of desired mobility.

Hips

The daily demands you place on your hips to bear weight, walk, climb stairs, bend and twist make them two of your hardest working joints. When weight loss, medications, limiting your activity and using a cane fail to provide relief, a hip operation may be the answer.

Osteotomy and joint resection are operations occasionally used to help reduce hip pain. Joint fusion is occasionally recommended for young people whose activity level may place too much stress on an artificial implant.

Pain relief and increased mobility are the hallmarks of a successful hip replacement. Also called total hip arthroplasty, this operation is by far the most successful for treating advanced arthritis of the hip.

Your hips are ball-and-socket joints. The large, round upper end of the thighbone (called the femoral head) fits into a cavity or socket (acetabulum) on the pelvic bone. This configuration makes swinging and rotating movements possible.

To mimic this design, the total hip implant consists of two main pieces: A metal shaft with a ball at the top end replaces the top of the thighbone (femur), and the socket of the pelvis also is replaced with a cup-shaped device typically made of a metal shell with an inner lining of plastic (polyethylene).

Surgeons typically recommend hip replacement for people older than 60 who have chronic debilitating pain and significant limitations of activities, although younger people are undergoing the procedure as it has become more reliable.

During the operation, the surgeon first removes the femoral head and prepares the pelvic socket by reaming it and then securing into it the new shell socket. Then the top end of the thighbone is drilled for insertion of the stem, which has an artificial ball at the end.

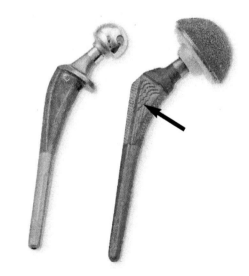

The artificial hip joint is designed to replace the natural ball-and-socket joint between the pelvis and thighbone (femur). *Left,* One type of implant is secured with cement. *Right,* The other type has a specially treated, porous component (*arrow*), which allows bone to grow into its surface.

Both the stem and the socket can be secured to the bone using either cemented or uncemented fixation. In cemented fixation, acrylic cement (polymethylmethacrylate) is used to fix the stem and the socket to the bone. This is similar to the cement used by dentists for artificial teeth. Uncemented fixation, on the other hand, uses devices that have special surfaces that promote bone ingrowth. This method of fixation takes a little longer to mature. No hard and fast rules dictate whether cemented or uncemented fixation should be used. In general, however, uncemented fixation is used in people under age 50 and cemented fixation is used for people over age 70. For people between ages 50 and 70, it's not uncommon for hybrid fixation to be used, in which the socket is fixed without cement and the stem is fixed with cement.

Fixation of the components doesn't seem to be the problem it once was. Today, both cemented and uncemented fixation can provide durable results for 20 years or more. As the longevity of hip replacements increases, other issues, including routine wear, become important. Newer materials are being tested to prolong the useful life of hip implants.

Knees

Your knee is an engineering marvel. More than a simple hinge, it has one of the widest ranges of motion of any joint in your body. It not only bends but also slides, glides and swivels. In addition, it absorbs the force of up to seven times your body's weight.

Several surgical options are available to relieve knee pain and restore mobility. Arthroscopic debridement is frequently used to repair cartilage tears or remove loose tissue fragments.

Synovectomy can decrease pain and swelling in people with rheumatoid arthritis whose cartilage is not significantly damaged. Because the knee joint is relatively large, surgeons typically use an arthroscope to perform this procedure. Using this device, the surgeon can view the joint and remove the diseased tissue with other instruments. Arthroscopic synovectomy requires a much smaller incision than a traditional operation, so recovery is much quicker.

Surgeons sometimes recommend osteotomy to slow cartilage damage in the knees and relieve pain. By trimming and repositioning the leg bones, they can distribute weight more evenly across your knee joint and correct curvature or bowing in the lower leg bones caused by osteoarthritis. Surgeons typically recommend this procedure for young, active people.

A hand for Laura

I used to make a living with my hands. I was a factory welder, making auto parts.

Nine-and-a-half years into the job, when I was 39, I woke up one spring morning with a foot aching horribly. I went to my family doctor, who diagnosed tendinitis and gave me steroids. But within a week, the pain had spread to joints throughout my body: both feet, hands, wrists, knees, everywhere. I went back to the doctor and said, "Tell me this isn't arthritis." For I was suffering from what I remember my grandmother had. My blood tested positive for rheumatoid arthritis.

I pushed myself at work and managed to hang on for 6 more months, long enough to qualify for a pension. But within 3 years after the pain had started, my hands had become nearly worthless. I remember going to the grocery store one day and not being able to open the door. It was too heavy. I turned around and cried all the way home.

Even drinking a glass of water became tough; I had to hold it with the heels of my hands. Eating out was too embarrassing. But with my family's help, I made adaptations around the house. My favorite was a foot pedal that opened the refrigerator. Another was a nail that my husband drove through a cutting board. I would stick a potato on the nail so that it wouldn't slip away when I cleaned or peeled it.

That's about the time I decided to replace the knuckle joints in all five fingers of my right hand. The doctor warned me that the new joints wouldn't work as well as the ones God gave me. But I sat there thinking that the ones God gave me didn't work at all.

It took a year before the fingers felt like they belonged to me. But now I have one hand that can do just about anything I need it to do. I can twist the key that starts the car — something I hadn't been able to do for years. I even hand painted a dozen sweat suits for Christmas presents.

Laura
Grand Rapids, Mich.

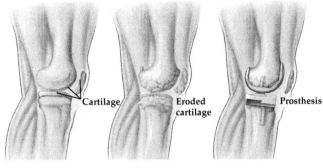

Knee replacement can restore function. The artificial joint has metal alloy caps for your thigh-bone and shinbone and high-density plastic to replace eroded cartilage within the joint and on your kneecap.

Cartilage

Eroded cartilage

Prosthesis

Healthy knee   **Osteoarthritic knee**   **Artificial knee**

Joint fusion is an option for people who aren't candidates for arthro-plasty. Even though fusion limits knee motion, it allows you to bear weight on your leg without pain.

Knee replacement, also known as total knee arthroplasty, helps about 230,000 Americans get back on their feet each year. The procedure has become as successful as hip replacement. Pain relief comes from replac-ing the diseased bone or tissue with the new knee parts.

Although most people who undergo knee replacement are age 60 or older, surgeons occasionally replace knees in people who are younger. However, the active lifestyles of younger people may cause greater wear and stress on the artificial knee, requiring it to be replaced in the future.

A knee prosthesis is made of metal alloy and high-density plastic and usually consists of several parts not directly connected to each other. One of the largest parts is made of metal alloy and attaches to the end of your femur where diseased bone has been removed.

Another major component, also of metal alloy, resembles a tray on a pedestal. The surgeon anchors the pedestal of the tray into the shaft of your shinbone. The platform of the tray has a surface of high-density plastic. It provides a resting place for the metal component attached to your femur. The plastic acts as the new joint's cartilage. The replacement may also include another small component — a circular piece of plastic that attaches to your kneecap to replace cartilage or diseased bone.

To prepare your knee for the prosthesis, your surgeon will remove the diseased bone and realign your existing connective tissues to hold the joint together after the prosthesis is in place. Leg bones damaged by arthritis also may need to be realigned.

Surgeons can use a bone cement (methylmethacrylate) or a cementless prosthesis. Mayo Clinic surgeons believe that cemented prostheses have less chance of early loosening and developing other problems. New methods of manufacturing and applying the cement also may improve outcomes.

Ankles and feet

Like your hips and knees, your ankles and feet are weight-bearing joints that help carry you through your day. Various operations are used to relieve pain and restore stability to these joints. Bone resection and repair of bunions or other bony growths in the feet can make walking and standing less painful.

Tendon repair and synovectomy also can provide relief before cartilage becomes badly eroded. If your symptoms are severe, your surgeon may recommend fusing bones in your feet or ankle to improve stability and reduce pain.

Ankle and foot joint replacements are still rather new procedures that aren't widely used, partly because they lack a strong record of success.

Your body's joints

Your body has several types of joints:

- *Fixed* — These joints don't move. They absorb shock to help prevent bones from breaking. Fixed joints in your skull protect sensitive brain tissue underneath.
- *Hinge* — Like the hinge in a doorway, your knee joints let you move forward and backward.
- *Pivot* — These joints allow a rotating movement. Your elbow has both hinge and pivot joints.
- *Ball-and-socket* — The large round end of a long bone fits into a hollow part of another bone. This makes swinging and rotating movements possible. You get the most movement from ball-and-socket joints in your hips and shoulders.

Preparing for your surgery

You and your surgeon will decide when you need to be admitted to the hospital before your operation. Planning for meals, housekeeping and other assistance can help you cope with the change in activity level you may experience after your operation.

Be sure to review your medications with your surgeon or family physician several weeks before your operation. Many surgeons ask their patients to discontinue the use of nonsteroidal anti-inflammatory drugs (NSAIDs) 1 or 2 weeks before the operation to minimize the risk of bleeding. Acetaminophen (Tylenol, others) or a COX-2 inhibitor can usually be substituted for pain control if necessary. If you're taking methotrexate or other similar drugs such as azathioprine (Imuran) or cyclosporine (Sandimmune, Neoral) for rheumatoid arthritis, your physician or surgeon probably will ask you to stop taking it 1 or 2 weeks before the operation to minimize the risk of infection. You can start again 1 or 2 weeks afterward.

Potential risks and complications

You'll be monitored closely during and after the procedure to prevent problems such as infection, blood loss, heart attack or a blood clot in the lung. Other rare but possible complications are nerve and blood vessel injury, joint dislocation, bone loss (with arthroplasty), and even death.

Joint operation often requires a blood transfusion. The vast majority of people who receive transfusions have no adverse reactions. Still, the safest blood is your own. Your immune system will not react to your blood, and you cannot give yourself an infection.

Use of a patient's own blood, also known as autologous transfusion, has become common. When planning an elective operation, you can donate your own blood ahead of time. Usually, you give it over a period of a few weeks in advance of your operation. Your blood is stored and used as necessary to replace blood lost during the operation.

Over the long term, the site of artificial joint implants is susceptible to infection. Each time you have dental work, oral or certain other types of surgery, a catheterization, or a bacterial infection, your doctor may prescribe a course of antibiotics to reduce the risk of implant infection.

Implants may also loosen or wear out with time, but improved designs and surgical techniques have prolonged the life of replacement joints. Rarely, an implanted artificial hip joint dislocates with certain movements or, more often, an injury. If you have rheumatoid arthritis in other joints, excessive stress on them in the postoperative period while you're protecting the operated joint may cause a flare-up.

Your hospital stay

The length of your hospital stay will depend on many factors, including the type of joint operation you have, your age and overall health and whether you experience any surgical complications.

After the procedure, your surgical care team will monitor your vital signs, alertness, and pain or comfort level and adjust your medications accordingly. Your doctor may prescribe antibiotics to prevent infection and anticoagulant medication to prevent blood clots.

Procedures that use only small incisions and local anesthesia, such as arthroscopic debridement and arthroscopic synovectomy, frequently do not require an overnight stay in the hospital.

In the 1960s, people stayed in bed for 2 to 3 weeks after a hip operation. Today, physical therapy begins almost immediately after most joint procedures, and hospital stays are shorter. Even though you may require assistance at first, you can probably expect to be up and out of your hospital bed several times daily. Remarkably, most people leave the hospital about 5 to 8 days after total joint replacement.

Rehabilitation

Exercise and rest are both important elements in recovery, so it's essential to follow the activity guidelines established by your surgeon or physical therapist. If you don't do your exercises, you can end up with a stiff, painful joint.

Physical therapists can help you learn the proper way to use and protect your new or altered joint. Exercise can improve joint motion, strengthen the muscles around your joint, reduce pain and help you improve your mobility. You may need to learn how to use assistive devices such as a walker or crutches to guard against falls or other injuries while your muscles and surgical site heal.

Occupational therapists can help you become independent in activities of daily living and instruct you in the use of assistive devices such as dressing aids, grab bars, a raised toilet seat and a bath bench. The goal of rehabilitation is for you to become as independent in your care and activities as possible.

Depending on your age, physical condition and home situation, your surgeon may recommend a short stay in a rehabilitation center to allow you to focus on your recovery before returning home.

Recovery at home

Continuing your recommended exercises at home will help you recover more quickly. Your doctor and physical therapist can tell you when you'll be able to return to your favorite activities and identify positions or activities to avoid. If your operation involved weight-bearing joints, you'll probably need to use crutches or a walker and then a cane for a while after you return to your home. If you have difficulty getting along at home, your doctor may recommend in-home visits by a physical or occupational therapist.

Joint infection may still be a risk after your dismissal from the hospital. Make sure you contact your physician if you have a fever, if your incision opens or if you notice any increase in pain, tenderness, swelling, redness, warmth or drainage near the surgical site. Also watch for signs of circulation problems near your joint, such as numbness or tingling, or changes in color or temperature in your limbs.

Life after recovery

Full recovery from a joint operation may take only a few weeks for some tendon, ligament or cartilage repairs. Some types of joint fusion, osteotomy or joint replacements can require a few months to a full year of recovery before your bones heal fully and you regain your strength, stability and mobility. But many people experience a reduction in pain and swelling, as well as easier movement, just days after the procedure. Your age, overall health and commitment to your rehabilitation program can play a role in how quickly you recover. Follow-up visits with your doctor also are important.

Although recovering from joint replacement may take time, implants give many people a new lease on life. Ten years after surgery, about 90 percent of those with knee replacement are pain-free and have experienced no breakdown of their new joint. After more than three decades, cemented hip implants also have a track record: About 85 percent of people can still walk comfortably 20 years after surgery.

Even with a successful joint operation, you may need to avoid high-impact activities such as running, downhill skiing or tennis. But, depending on which joint was affected, you should be able to resume an active, full life.

Chapter 9

Complementary and alternative treatments

Conventional medicine has much to offer in helping you manage your arthritis. But you may have heard about methods or treatments that weren't discussed in previous chapters. Maybe you saw a news report or advertisement about a product promising pain-free joints. Or perhaps a friend told you she's taking a vitamin or herbal preparation that makes her feel better.

What you've probably heard about are forms of complementary and alternative medicine. Complementary medicine has been described as unconventional treatments used in addition to treatments by your doctor. Alternative medicine has been described as treatments used in place of traditional medicine. More recently, complementary and alternative medicine have been defined as therapies that encompass a broad range of approaches to enhancing health or healing that are not widely taught in American medical schools, not generally used in hospitals and not usually reimbursed by health insurance companies. Some complementary and alternative medicine approaches share some basic principles with Western medicine, but others do not.

Americans spend more than $1 billion a year on unconventional treatments for arthritis. Why are these unorthodox therapies so compelling? The lack of a cure with many conventional arthritis medicines and the side effects associated with some treatments, especially after long-term use, undoubtedly lead some people to seek alternatives.

Because many complementary and alternative medicine methods haven't been studied extensively by researchers using mainstream scientific methods, it's difficult for the scientific community to evaluate their effectiveness or safety. And with much of today's research funding coming from the pharmaceutical industry, some low-tech, nontraditional approaches to managing diseases such as arthritis may not get as much attention from the research community as they deserve. For these reasons, many Western physicians just don't know enough about these methods to endorse them. Nonetheless, a growing body of evidence indicates that complementary and alternative medicine practices could have a role in treating and managing some diseases.

Options available

Acupuncture

This 2,500-year-old Chinese medical treatment involves inserting hair-thin needles under your skin to stimulate specific points that allow the free flow of qi, sometimes written chi (pronounced chee), the Chinese word for energy or life force. Traditional acupuncturists believe that pain is reduced and health is restored when qi flows without obstruction along pathways called meridians that run throughout your body.

During a typical session, an acupuncturist inserts anywhere from 1 to 40 metal needles for 15 to 40 minutes. The acupuncturist may also manipulate the needles manually or by electrical stimulation or heat.

Scientific research indicates that acupuncture stimulates your body's own morphine-like painkilling chemicals called endorphins. For this reason, acupuncture may be particularly appealing to people who can't tolerate side effects associated with long-term use of nonsteroidal anti-inflammatory drugs (NSAIDs). A growing body of evidence seems to support acupuncture in certain situations. For example, the National Institutes of Health found that acupuncture may be a reasonable pain management option for osteoarthritis. However, a more recent report by the American College of Rheumatology found that acupuncture works no better than a placebo.

How often you require treatment and how many sessions you'll have depend on your practitioner and your symptoms.

Used more widely in Asia than in the United States, acupuncture is not well understood by many Western physicians. Some are skeptical about the effectiveness of acupuncture because research has shown that some people also experience pain relief regardless of where the needles are placed. In addition, there are no physical structures in the body corresponding to the so-called meridians. Future research may better define which people or types of arthritis are most likely to benefit from acupuncture.

Acupuncture is generally a low-risk treatment, but it's important to find a skilled practitioner who uses sterile needles.

Aromatherapy

This ancient form of healing uses oils derived from plant extracts and resins to promote both health and beauty. Practitioners believe these oils can help treat various illnesses, including arthritis pain and inflammation, when massaged into your skin or inhaled. Used more widely in Europe than in the United States, aromatherapy treatments and products are sometimes found in stores that sell natural health products.

Although it's true that many modern medications have come from plant extracts, more study is needed to determine whether any added medicinal benefits are associated with the plant oils used in aromatherapy.

Bee venom therapy

The belief that honeybee venom has curative powers has been around for centuries. Some people theorize that bee venom has enzymes that relieve the symptoms of rheumatoid arthritis by fighting inflammation. Another hypothesis is that bee venom causes your body to increase its production of steroids, which may help relieve symptoms.

During this treatment, bees are applied to the arthritic joint or joints, allowed to sting and then removed. Some people also have tried injecting purified bee venom under the skin near problem joints. It's not known how many people use this treatment. Some beekeepers perform bee venom therapy (BVT), and some people purchase bees or bee venom and treat themselves.

Because there's little scientific research into the use of BVT for arthritis in humans, it's unclear how much venom or how many stings are necessary to relieve the symptoms of arthritis. Some European scientists using injections of purified bee venom have documented relief of symptoms in small groups of animals and people.

Because up to 15 percent of the population can have mild to even fatal allergic reactions to insect venom, this treatment is risky for some people. Large studies involving people (clinical trials) may help shed light on whether bee venom or one of its components can play a role in the treatment of arthritis.

Biofeedback

This relaxation method uses technology to teach you how to control certain bodily functions to help you control arthritis pain.

During a biofeedback session, you use relaxation techniques such as meditation and guided imagery to calm yourself. Various machines monitor and give you feedback on your bodily functions, such as heart rate, breathing patterns, body temperature and muscle activity. The goals of this feedback are to teach you how to lower your body temperature, slow your breathing and heart rate and relax your muscles so that you can enter a relaxed state in which you can cope better with the pain. Some biofeedback techniques are taught in physical therapy or behavioral medicine departments in hospitals and medical centers.

Copper bracelets

For decades, some people have advocated wearing copper bracelets to help fight arthritis pain. They theorize that small amounts of copper pass through your skin and neutralize free radicals, toxic molecules that damage cells.

Although wearing copper jewelry is probably harmless, most doctors find little basis on which to recommend it as a therapy for arthritis because scientific research supporting its effectiveness is scarce. The only known side effect is discolored skin.

Dimethyl sulfoxide

Dimethyl sulfoxide (DMSO) is an industrial solvent, similar to turpentine, that is sold in some health food stores as a treatment of arthritis. Some people believe that DMSO can relieve pain and reduce swelling when rubbed on the skin.

More than 20 years of medical research with DMSO has yielded conflicting results. DMSO isn't approved by the Food and Drug Administration (FDA) for human use, except for treating a rare type of bladder inflammation. Some studies using animals found that joints treated with DMSO actually showed more inflammatory changes than untreated joints.

Industrial-strength DMSO (sold in hardware stores) may contain poisonous contaminants. For these reasons, arthritis experts don't recommend using this solvent as a treatment of arthritis.

Glucosamine and chondroitin

There's preliminary evidence that the dietary supplements glucosamine and chondroitin can help maintain existing cartilage and stimulate new cartilage growth. In November 1999, Belgian researchers presented a study to the American College of Rheumatology showing that glucosamine appears to slow the progression of osteoarthritis of the knee. Researchers from Boston University School of Medicine analyzed several published articles using glucosamine and chondroitin preparations and concluded that they're likely to provide some relief of osteoarthritis symptoms.

Research is ongoing, and more information regarding the effectiveness of these supplements should be available within a few years. The National Institutes of Health is sponsoring a 4-year study begun in 2000 in which glucosamine and chondroitin are being used to treat more than 1,500 people with osteoarthritis of the knee.

In the meantime, you should exercise caution. Data regarding the efficacy, tolerability and toxicity of these supplements are still being gathered. If you have an allergy to shellfish, you shouldn't take glucosamine because it's derived from the shells of these animals. There is anecdotal information that glucosamine may aggravate diabetes by increasing insulin resistance or decreasing insulin production, leading to elevated blood glucose levels. In addition, if you take a prescription blood thinner, chondroitin may affect its levels.

Gold rings

Joint damage caused by rheumatoid arthritis is typically affects the same joint on both sides of the body. That's why some experts took note of a study that found exceptions to that rule. Researchers in England observed that some people with rheumatoid arthritis who wore a gold ring on one hand lacked this symmetrical deterioration in the joint nearest the ring.

This observation suggests that the skin may be able to absorb enough gold to delay joint damage. Injections of gold salts have long been prescribed to reduce inflammation and slow disease progression. Large studies will be necessary to confirm this theory and determine whether it has any broader applications in the treatment of arthritis.

Guided imagery

Also called visualization, guided imagery is a technique in which you relax by calling up an image you experience with your senses.

Imagining something stimulates the same parts of your brain that are affected when you actually experience what you're imagining. The message your brain receives from your imagination is sent to other brain centers and to the systems in your body that regulate key functions, such as heart rate and blood pressure. This may help alleviate pain and other physical symptoms, reducing your need for pain medications.

Herbal treatments

Herbs are the basis for many conventional medicines, such as aspirin, morphine and digitalis. And scientists continue to discover new medicines derived from plants. Outside traditional medicine, herbal preparations are gaining popularity for treating both rheumatoid arthritis and osteoarthritis. Herbs and other plant extracts, both exotic and common, are now sold as alternative pain relievers and inflammation fighters.

Cinnamon, ginger, celery, evening primrose oil, devil's claw, feverfew, stinging nettle, avocado and soy extracts, yucca and dandelion are among the herbs used in preparations that have received attention for their potential to relieve the symptoms of arthritis. Traditional Chinese healers have used extracts from a plant called thunder god vine (*Tripterygium wilfordii*) to treat various autoimmune diseases, including rheumatoid arthritis. Scientists still need to identify the possible active components in this plant. Research conducted in the United States has suggested that one or more such components, including gamma linolenic acid, may have some potential benefit. Many parts of this plant are toxic and may cause death if eaten.

Given the past success of medications derived from plants, research may someday help carve a niche for herbal treatments in the fight against arthritis symptoms. Many herbs contain powerful substances that can be toxic or interfere with medications. Because herbal products is not regulated by the FDA before they go on the market, it's difficult to tell which herbs have been proved effective and how to use these herbs safely. For these reasons, talk to your doctor before you take any herbal preparation.

Homeopathic treatments

Homeopathy was developed by German physician Samuel Hahnemann in the late 18th century and is practiced around the globe. According to Hahnemann's law of similars, if a substance causes you to develop certain symptoms when you're healthy, a small dose of this substance can treat illnesses with similar symptoms. During an evaluation, a classic homeopath may ask questions about your physical, mental and emotional symptoms before prescribing treatment. Most homeopathic treatments are extremely diluted preparations of natural substances, such as plants and minerals.

Scientific research hasn't yet explained how homeopathic medicines might work. Because most homeopathic medicines are so diluted they contain virtually no molecules of the active substances, many modern scientists are skeptical about their effectiveness.

Although traditional medical training isn't required, some homeopaths are physicians or other types of licensed health care providers, such as chiropractors, nurses and pharmacists. Regulation and licensure vary from state to state.

Hypnosis

This induced state of relaxation enhances your focus and makes you more open to act on suggestions given to you, or that you give yourself, when you're in a hypnotic state. Once you're trained to self-hypnotize, you can use this technique to help manage your pain or shift your attention away from it.

No one's sure how hypnosis works. There is evidence that it alters your brain wave patterns in much the same way as other relaxation techniques.

About 80 percent of adults can be hypnotized. Learning this technique requires motivation and patience.

Joint manipulations

Some complementary or alternative medicine practitioners such as chiropractors and osteopaths use joint manipulation to relieve the symptoms of osteoarthritis. These practitioners claim that manipulation can relax the tissues surrounding joints and improve circulation and joint mobility. Several methods are used.

In general, the gentle stretching and massage that sometimes accompany manipulation can be therapeutic if performed by a skilled practitioner. However, it's unclear whether joint manipulation or realignment of the spine also helps relieve joint pain caused by osteoarthritis. If you have rheumatoid arthritis, avoid neck manipulations.

Magnets

Some people believe that magnets can play a role in the healing process and in controlling their pain. As with any new therapy, many people are claiming results. But so far reports are mainly anecdotal. Although research may someday find magnet therapy to be beneficial, to date there's little medical evidence to back up health claims, and the therapy is still considered experimental.

Most of the claims you see or hear regarding the "healing power" of magnets are from manufacturers of alternative health products. They've incorporated magnets into products such as arm and leg wraps, belts, mattress pads, necklaces and shoe inserts, claiming the products can relieve various health problems. However, there's no scientific evidence that magnets used in this manner work.

Researchers are just starting to look at magnets as a possible therapy for some forms of chronic pain, including pain associated with arthritis, injury and post-polio syndrome. Some of the studies do suggest benefits, but more research is needed regarding proper and effective use of the devices and who may be a candidate for such therapy. Some researchers believe that inappropriate use of magnet therapy may actually lead to health problems.

Meditation

This technique helps you enter a deeply restful state that reduces your body's stress response. You can meditate by sitting quietly and focusing on your breathing or a mantra, a simple sound repeated over and over. You can also meditate while walking or jogging.

Regular practice of meditation such as yoga can help relax breathing, slow brain waves and decrease muscle tension and heart rate. It can also lessen your body's response to the chemicals it produces when you're stressed by pain.

Nutritional supplements

New claims for vitamin and mineral supplements are in the news almost every day. Vitamins A, C and E, called antioxidants, are being studied as a possible treatment of arthritis because they may help prevent cell damage that leads to joint pain.

Cold-water-fish oils also are gaining popularity for their ability to fight the inflammation caused by rheumatoid arthritis. Some research suggests that omega-3 fatty acids from cold-water fish (salmon, mackerel, herring) may give modest, temporary relief from inflammation and help some people reduce their need for NSAIDs.

Soybean and avocado oils also are being researched as possible treatments of osteoarthritis. One group of researchers noted that some people who consumed supplements containing these oils, particularly people with osteoarthritis of the hip, reported a reduction in their arthritis symptoms and their need for NSAIDs.

Future research will explore more fully whether boosting your intake of these or any other supplements is a safe or effective way to prevent arthritis or relieve its symptoms.

SAM-e

S-adenosyl-methionine (SAM-e) is another supplement that has gained a lot of attention as a possible therapy for osteoarthritis. Pronounced "SAM-ee," this compound occurs naturally in all human tissue and organs. Among other functions, it helps produce and regulate hormones and cell membranes. SAM-e has been used in Europe for years as a prescription medication for arthritis and depression. In March 1999, it became available in the United States as an over-the-counter supplement.

SAM-e has been studied in a number of clinical trials, which have shown it may relieve osteoarthritic pain as effectively as NSAIDs and with fewer side effects. Manufacturers of SAM-e also claim that it can regenerate cartilage in damaged joints, but currently no scientific evidence supports this. As with other supplements, more studies will help determine the effectiveness of SAM-e in treating arthritis, its safety and possible side effects.

Snake venom

Snake venom has piqued the interest of both conventional and complementary and alternative medicine practitioners. The powerful effect of some snake venoms on the nervous system and their triggering of other side effects have made some researchers hopeful that medicine can adapt these powers for therapeutic purposes.

Currently, no FDA approved arthritis medications are derived from snake venom. There's also little scientific data that support its use in treating arthritis. Because of the toxicity of snake venom, arthritis experts warn that more research is needed to determine whether it can play a role in treating arthritis.

Words of caution

It's easy to become frustrated by the limitations of conventional medicine to treat arthritis. You may believe any possible cure is better than none.

But if you opt for complementary or alternative medicine approaches, do so with knowledge of both their potential benefits and risks.

Many people turn to complementary or alternative medicine therapies because they believe they're safer or more natural than the approaches offered by traditional medicine. It's true that many conventional medical and surgical treatments have some significant side effects and health risks. However, the same can be said about some complementary and alternative medicine approaches. As noted throughout this chapter, evaluating the effectiveness or safety of complementary and alternative treatments can be difficult because many haven't been studied extensively by researchers using mainstream scientific methods.

The conventional form of medicine practiced by most doctors is grounded in scientific method that relies on experimentation and established research methods. Before a new treatment becomes widely accepted, scientists typically publish their results in established scientific journals. These journals are reviewed by other experts who aren't associated with the experiment or the sale of the product.

Reviewers try to objectively evaluate the validity of the findings and point out any problems with the method of study or conclusions made from the results of the experimental trials. Through this process, researchers and their reviewers attempt to identify the health benefits and risks associated with a new treatment. The scientific method also attempts to distinguish effective treatments from ineffective treatments enhanced by the so-called placebo effect. This phenomenon causes some people to feel better simply because they're receiving treatment of any kind, whether it's a sugar pill or a real medication.

The cyclic nature of rheumatoid arthritis also can make it difficult to gauge the effectiveness of a given treatment. Because flares and remissions can occur spontaneously (for reasons that are unclear), you may be tempted to credit relief of symptoms to whatever treatment you recently tried. This type of "coincidental cure" can be misleading and make any treatment appear more effective than it actually is. Symptoms in osteoarthritis also can vary for reasons that are unclear. Changes may occur after a joint is used more strenuously than usual, or there may be no recognizable cause. Evaluation of therapy, whether conventional, or complementary or alternative, can be challenging because of these variations.

Another important fact about complementary and alternative medicine is that it is largely an unregulated industry. Unlike pharmaceutical or over-the-counter medicines, herbal preparations, vitamins and other nutritional supplements aren't evaluated or approved by the FDA prior to being placed on the market. This means they are sold without being tested for safety or effectiveness. Similarly, some complementary and alternative medicine practitioners don't need a license or other proof of competency to perform their trade.

This limited regulation also makes it easier for unscrupulous or fraudulent practitioners and businesses to prey on people who are desperate for a cure at any cost.

How to evaluate complementary medicine

The National Center for Complementary and Alternative Medicine (NCCAM) is part of the National Institutes of Health. NCCAM advises consumers to take several steps before trying any complementary or alternative therapy.

1. Talk to your doctor. Some treatments can interfere with medications you may be taking or affect other health conditions you may have. This conversation may not be easy if your doctor is skeptical about complementary and alternative medicine practices. But good communication with your physician is essential, particularly if you're taking medications or undergoing other treatments.

2. Research what's known about the safety and effectiveness of any complementary or alternative therapy. This means finding out about the advantages and disadvantages, risks, side effects, expected results and length of treatment. You can start by asking your doctor or searching for

Basics of scientific research

The randomized controlled trial is basic to most medical research designed to evaluate a new medication or other form of treatment. In this type of study, participants are randomly divided into two or more groups. One group receives the new therapy and one receives a placebo — a substance with no known effect on the condition being studied. Throughout the study, neither the participant nor the physician knows who received the therapy being tested. With this approach, the results are objective.

objective scientific literature in your public library or university library, from the NCCAM or through reliable sources on the Internet. The NCCAM Web address is *www.nccam.nih.gov.*

You can also talk to other people with arthritis who have tried the treatment, even though they may be a less objective source of information. Remember that their testimonials can't prove how safe or effective the treatment will be for you.

3. Research the expertise of the practitioner or salesperson associated with a given treatment. Just as you do when you choose a doctor, you'll want to examine the professional competence of anyone who offers you a complementary or alternative treatment. If you're working with a licensed practitioner, check with your local and state medical boards for information about credentials and whether any complaints have been filed against him or her.

If you're buying a product from a business, check with your local or state business bureau to find out whether any complaints have been filed against the company.

4. Estimate the total cost of the treatment. Because many complementary and alternative approaches aren't covered by health insurance, it's essential to understand all of the costs associated with a treatment.

5. Don't substitute an unproven alternative treatment for one that has been proved effective. Don't stop use of your medications or treatments on your own.

Make no assumptions

Complementary and alternative medicine is a fast-growing field that may offer some new approaches to treating arthritis. However, because the products and services are part of an industry with limited regulatory oversight, you can't assume their safety and effectiveness. Become informed about the possible risks and benefits associated with a given treatment before you act. Then talk to your doctor and think it over carefully.

Chapter 10

Promising trends in treatment

I t's true that no one seems to be on the brink of discovering a cure for arthritis. It's also no secret that many of the treatments used to relieve the symptoms of arthritis can have limited benefits and significant side effects.

The good news is that researchers are beginning to paint a clearer picture of what triggers the symptoms of arthritis and causes them to continue. Although a cure isn't in sight, scientists are making significant progress in several key areas of research.

There have been major advances in the last few years in understanding the interaction between certain cells and joints that leads to inflammation. Inflammation is responsible for much of the pain and damage that occurs with rheumatoid arthritis and is also present in osteoarthritis.

Chemical messengers among cells are called cytokines (SI-to-keenz). Inhibiting cytokines that have a role in inflammation and increasing cytokines that suppress inflammation will continue to be important in developing new approaches to treating rheumatoid arthritis. Targeting cytokines that contribute to the breakdown of cartilage, as well as the use of growth factors that promote healthy cartilage cells, will likely be part of the strategy for treating osteoarthritis.

Medications

Drugs that block joint damage and inflammation

Researchers continue to look for new medications that can more effectively prevent inflammation and joint damage — without the serious side effects of some drugs currently in use.

The introduction in recent years of biologic agents for the treatment of rheumatoid arthritis has shown promise. These agents inhibit the cytokines interleukin-1 (IL-1) and tumor necrosis factor-alpha (TNF-alpha), both of which play a role in causing inflammation. The use of these agents is associated with reduced symptoms in rheumatoid arthritis, and these drugs can limit joint damage and improve function as well. Other cytokine inhibitors are expected to be developed.

Agents that promote or replace cytokines that have an anti-inflammatory effect also may become available. Novel strategies of cytokine manipulation may involve gene therapy that uses DNA to prompt the body to produce beneficial cytokines and to change the balance of these chemical messengers to inhibit the inflammatory process.

The use of new drugs in combination with currently available drugs may allow for greater control of rheumatoid arthritis. The number of

Here's a term you may hear more about

Is controlling the growth of blood vessels a key to the treatment of rheumatoid arthritis? Maybe.

Angiogenesis (an-je-o-JEN-uh-sis) is the term used to describe the process of blood vessel growth. Several researchers are trying to understand and better control this complex process.

Most of the recent work has focused on cancer. Tumors can't grow to life-threatening size unless they're adequately nourished by blood. Therefore, they give off substances called angiogenic factors that promote the growth of tiny blood vessels.

In rheumatoid arthritis, excessive growth of blood vessels contributes to joint damage. By developing drugs that control blood vessel growth, the damage may be avoided or minimized.

In the future, *anti-angiogenesis* is a term you may be hearing as a strategy for treating cancer, rheumatoid arthritis, psoriasis and eye diseases such as glaucoma and retinitis pigmentosa.

possible drug combinations increases with each new drug that's approved. Overall, drug therapies for arthritis are targeting those parts of the inflammation process and the immune system that are responsible for disease while at the same time interfering less with the normal immune system functions.

Antibiotics

Scientists continue to explore the possibility that some form of infection might trigger the onset of rheumatoid arthritis. If so, perhaps taking a certain antibiotic might prevent the disease. Building on this theory, researchers are testing whether antibiotics can suppress progression of the disease and relieve symptoms.

Most of the common forms of inflammatory arthritis are not caused by the presence of bacteria in the joint. Still, research has shown that some antibiotics may be helpful in some forms of arthritis because they suppress enzymes and other proteins known to cause inflammation.

Minocycline is an antibiotic that also may help people who have early rheumatoid arthritis. Commonly used to treat acne, minocycline seems to provide a measure of relief from joint swelling, stiffness and pain. Like its cousin doxycycline, minocycline is an antibiotic that seems to block enzymes (called metalloproteinases) that destroy cartilage inside your joints. Researchers believe that drugs like minocycline that more effectively block enzymes which cause tissue damage may slow or prevent joint damage that occurs in both osteoarthritis and rheumatoid arthritis.

Future research will be needed to determine whether these medications work because of their antibiotic activity or because of some other process. Who can benefit most from them must also be determined as well as how to use them safely with other arthritis medications.

Preventive vaccines

A certain type of white blood cell, called a T cell, or T lymphocyte, may initiate an immune system response that eventually leads to joint destruction in rheumatoid arthritis. If so, a vaccine might suppress the activity of these T cells and prevent rheumatoid arthritis.

T cell vaccines have been tested on animals with various immune disorders. The specific types of T cell malfunction that occur in people with rheumatoid arthritis remain to be understood. In addition, vaccines that give rise to antibodies that block peptides that promote inflammation also are being developed.

Estrogen replacement therapy

Estrogen replacement therapy (ERT) has been used for years to help reduce the risk of osteoporosis. Researchers report that women who use ERT may also be protecting themselves against osteoarthritis of the hip. A study of more than 4,000 women found that those taking ERT had a lower risk of hip osteoarthritis than those who weren't.

Because osteoarthritis becomes so prevalent after menopause, when levels of estrogen dwindle, doctors have long suspected that estrogen depletion may play a role in the development of this disease. Although researchers don't know why it's protective, they suspect that estrogen modifies factors involved in the natural buildup and breakdown of bone and cartilage.

Genes

Genes are the part of your chromosomes that determine your hair color, height, eye color and most other characteristics. Researchers are learning to single out genes that make people more susceptible to arthritis and those that fight this disease. Does having these genetic defects guarantee you'll get arthritis? No. Genes appear to be only one of many factors responsible for causing the disease. However, it's important to determine how common these defects are and whether they can be prevented.

Once researchers have pinpointed a problem gene, they hope to develop a test to determine who's at risk of arthritis. This testing may encourage people to take steps to minimize their risks and seek medical treatment earlier. Many doctors believe that early diagnosis and treatment are crucial tools in preventing permanent joint damage.

Gene therapy

Specific genes may direct cells in your body to manufacture substances that help reduce inflammation, affect your body's immune responses or help protect your joints. The goal of gene therapy is to increase production of these natural enemies of arthritis. These genes might stop the inflammation of the joint lining, prevent breakdown of cartilage or stimulate the growth of more cartilage cells. For some diseases, gene therapy means supplying a healthy gene to the body to replace the defective gene or inserting genetic information into a defective gene to make it "healthy." In treating other diseases, gene therapy may involve blocking the action of a harmful gene.

Much of this research is still in the early stages. Although researchers have identified some of these helpful genes, they have yet to figure out the best method for delivering their protective benefits. Arthritis experts are hopeful that this type of treatment may have fewer side effects than existing medications.

Surgery

Advances in surgical procedures to treat arthritis are taking many directions. Joint replacement continues to improve with the development of components designed to last longer and loosen less often.

Improved techniques allow surgeons to more effectively treat problem joints by removing inflamed synovial tissue (arthroscopic synovectomy). And researchers are gaining a better understanding of how the body repairs damaged cartilage.

In cartilage transplantation, cartilage cells are removed from one of your healthy joints, grown in a laboratory and then inserted into a damaged joint along with a solution that stimulates growth.

Physicians are now using cartilage transplantation to treat only small areas of damaged cartilage. The ability to repair larger areas is likely to be developed in the next 5 to 10 years. Identifying and producing substances that stimulate healthy cartilage growth (cartilage growth factors) may help advance this technique.

Preliminary research into other forms of cartilage transplantation is also under way. A procedure called periosteal transplantation is showing promise. The periosteum is a thick membrane covering the surface of the bone, which is also responsible for making cartilage cells before birth. In this transplantation procedure, surgeons insert healthy periosteal cells into the damaged joint. When successful, the transplanted cells transform and again start to regenerate smooth cartilage and heal the damaged joint surface.

Surgeons at Mayo Clinic have been involved in periosteal transplantation research for several years. Currently, this technique can be successfully performed in only young people with limited areas of arthritis, for example, after an injury to a joint. This form of transplantation isn't used to treat people whose joints are damaged by chronic arthritis.

In people with early osteoarthritis affecting the knee, surgeons can insert a saucer-shaped metal spacer between worn parts of the joint, providing better alignment. This procedure is less invasive than total knee replacement.

Lifestyle

Nutrition

Eating a wide variety of foods and maintaining a healthy weight can help you cope with arthritis. For example, if you're overweight, studies have shown that losing weight will provide help to slow the progression of osteoarthritis of the knee, for any lower-extremity joint problems and for arthritis in your back. Loss of excessive weight has the potential to reduce pain and improve function and mobility. Although certain foods aren't proved to cause or prevent arthritis, vitamins and other nutrients in fruits and vegetables have attracted attention from physicians.

Antioxidants are vitamins found naturally in your body and in certain foods such as fruits and vegetables. These vitamins can neutralize potentially harmful substances called free radicals that result from your cells' ordinary metabolism. Some scientists believe damage from free radicals may contribute to disorders such as arthritis, cancer and cardiovascular disease.

Can you prevent arthritis or slow the progression of this disease by boosting your intake of antioxidants? One published report observed that people with rheumatoid arthritis had low levels of vitamins C and E and two forms of vitamin A (called retinol and beta carotene) before their disease developed. Another study suggested that a high intake of vitamins C and E and beta carotene may reduce your risk of developing osteoarthritis in the knees, slow its progression and reduce knee pain.

Larger studies may help prove these health claims and determine how much of these vitamins you'll need to prevent or treat arthritis.

Exercise

For years, doctors have assumed that muscle weakness occurs gradually when joint pain caused by osteoarthritis slows people down. Some researchers are flipping that equation. They suggest that weak quadriceps muscles, the muscles on the front of your thigh, may put you at risk of developing osteoarthritis of the knee. If this is true, exercises to strengthen quadriceps muscles may actually prevent progression of knee degeneration. To prove this theory, researchers are re-examining the role of muscle-strengthening exercises in preventing osteoarthritis.

Chapter 11

Traveling with arthritis

T ravel can be stressful even when you're healthy. But if you have arthritis, the thought of simple activities such as carrying luggage, changing planes or walking long distances can be enough to give you second thoughts about traveling.

But because you have arthritis doesn't mean that you're sentenced to a life of immobility. In fact, today it's easier to travel with a disability — either for business or pleasure — than ever before. Laws such as the Americans With Disabilities Act and the Air Carrier Access Act have nudged travel suppliers, from airlines to hotels to cruise ships, into making travel easier and more accessible for people who need special help. In addition, a range of new and established companies have recognized a growing market in catering to clients who have mildly to severely limited abilities, with operators developing special tours, vacation packages and activities for people with arthritis.

Of course, there are steps you, too, can take to make any trip more pleasurable.

Planning your trip

Where in the world do you want to go? Maybe you long to see Rome's Sistine Chapel or to hike the Na Pali Coast in Hawaii. Or maybe your company just needs you to solve a problem in Cleveland. The key to any successful trip starts with planning. With the right research, the world is yours for the exploring.

Naturally, you must be honest about your capabilities. Rock climbing might not be the best choice for someone with hip and knee limitations. A mountaintop helicopter excursion, though, might be an alternative. White-water rafting could be extremely painful with a neck condition. A week in a riverside cabin, though, might let you appreciate the water without discomfort.

Choose a vacation that allows you to be flexible. Consider how you'll spend a day alone if your travel companions plan more strenuous activities or extensive sightseeing. Remember, frequent rest periods may be the most important ingredient for a satisfying trip.

You can get a better idea of where you want to travel by preparing for your trip carefully. Send for information from the places you want to visit. Query tour companies that offer vacations that appeal to you. Read travel guides, including those geared toward people with disabilities, such as

---

Should you buy trip insurance?

Although some hotels and airlines will refund your money if you become ill — be sure to send a doctor's statement with your refund request — it's probably best to purchase trip cancellation insurance for expensive trips if you think there's a chance you'll be unable to travel. The policies are available from your travel agent or tour operator.

Review your medical insurance coverage before you go. Insurance policies sometimes include costs of medical illness while you're away from home, including travel back home if you become ill, but many plans don't include this coverage. Some policies exclude pre-existing conditions, so be certain to read the fine print. The AAA, formerly known as the American Automobile Association, offers low-cost trip insurance that's available even to non-members. The *Consumer Reports Travel Letter* is a good source of information about this and other travel topics.

Fodor's Great American Vacations for Travelers With Disabilities or any of the access guides).

Conversations with people who've taken similar trips can help you decide where you want to go and what you can expect when you arrive. And get your doctor's advice when planning a trip. He or she will have a good idea of what you can handle and how you can accomplish your travel goals.

Do you need a professional?

Many people rely on travel agents and tour operators. In most cases agents don't charge for their services, and these professionals can save you time and money. Tour operators generally combine several travel components, such as airfare, hotels and ground transportation, into one package that is usually less expensive than what you'd pay if you put them together yourself. The fees of tour operators are usually included in these expenses.

To select a travel agent, start by asking friends and relatives for referrals. You can also call agencies and ask about their experience in arranging trips for travelers with physical limitations. Choose an agent with whom you're comfortable discussing your particular needs, and make sure he or she is willing to spend the extra time on your individual arrangements. Treat your agent as a travel partner who wants to work for you after you've made the decisions about what you want and need.

Some travelers steer clear of group tours, but many people with arthritis find these a convenient and enjoyable way to travel. For the most part, the arrangements are handled for you, as are your bags, meals and transportation. One of the many tours designed for people with limited mobility may suit you best, because they're slower paced and allow for ample free time. In addition, tours for senior citizens generally take in fewer sights at a more leisurely pace. In either case read the details carefully to be sure you select the tour that's right for you.

Booking a hotel

Where you sleep at night can make or break a vacation or business trip, so keep your physical needs in mind when choosing lodging. Many large hotel chains publish free directories that describe special accommodations, but be sure to specify what you'll require well in advance. And always get written confirmation of any guaranteed arrangements.

You'll want to ask other things about where you'll be staying. For example, find out how close you'll be to the convention center, restaurant, pool or beach, where the elevators are located, whether bathrooms have handrails, whether the hotel shuttle can be used by someone with physical limitations and whether the doors and faucets have levers instead of hard-to-grasp knobs. You may also want to know about the availability of laundry and room services, and about handicapped parking, fire exits and access ramps.

In many cases hotels are equipped to offer a range of special amenities and services, such as city tours in accessible vans, heating pads for those unexpected flare-ups or in-house spas with whirlpools. According to the Society for Accessible Travel and Hospitality, it pays to ask as many questions as possible before you book.

And you're not limited to the major hotel chains either. An increasing number of bed-and-breakfasts, inns and other alternative accommodations now host travelers with disabilities. Most bed-and-breakfast guides include designations to indicate accessible rooms, or you can call InnSeekers toll-free at 888-INN-SEEK (888-466-7335) for information on accessible bed-and-breakfasts.

What to take along

Remember to pack light. It's good advice for all travelers, but especially for people with arthritis. This means you'll need to plan carefully so that you can satisfy whatever clothing changes you need, plus have all of the important items that make your arthritis more manageable. Don't forget to bring any aids you use daily, such as a raised toilet seat, long-handled reachers, special pillows or a heating pad. If you have electrical appliances or aids and are traveling to a foreign country, you may need to pack a plug or voltage adapter.

Use lightweight luggage with wheels or shoulder straps that make it easier to move. Check to see if porters and taxicabs will be available where you'll need them. Ask porters and taxicab drivers to carry your luggage whenever possible. At the airport, check your bags at the curb. Be sure to carry small bills for tipping people who assist you.

Always check the climate for your destination to decide what type of clothing will be most appropriate. Anything that can be layered lets you adapt easily to weather changes. In most cases loose clothing that allows maximal freedom of movement is best. Sunscreen, sunglasses, a wide-brimmed hat and comfortable shoes also are essential.

When packing medications, take more than enough to last through your trip, and carry them in their original containers. It's best to transport medicines in your carry-on luggage in case you're separated from the bags you've checked, although some travelers pack duplicates in their luggage. If you need medications kept cool, most train and airline personnel will gladly put them in the refrigerator, although you may prefer to carry them in a vacuum flask or similar container.

Along with your medications, bring copies of your prescriptions, your doctor's name and telephone and fax numbers, a summary of your medical history and a list of your medications. It's a good idea to leave a copy of this information at home with a friend or relative in case your doctor is unavailable. You also might consider wearing a medical alert bracelet or necklace if you have other medical problems in addition to arthritis.

Essential packing tips

- Pack as little as possible. Lay out the essentials, then leave half of them at home.

- Use lightweight luggage with sturdy wheels, a telescoping handle and a shoulder strap. This gives you maximum flexibility. Even if you don't take the baggage with you into the passenger compartment, carry-on luggage with wheels is practical and lightweight and can help you limit the amount of things you take along.

- Bring a pillow if you have neck problems. You can buy small ones that fit inside your luggage, or roll up a towel to fit your neck and tape the loose end.

- Lotion, oils and menthol gels are great for quick self-massages between sightseeing activities.

- Most U.S. airlines allow just one or two carry-on bags.

- Airlines allow two pieces of checked luggage. Medical equipment, such as wheelchairs, spare batteries, battery chargers and necessary supplies, isn't included in the limit and is transported at no extra charge. Just be sure that bags or boxes contain medical supplies and nothing else.

Traveling by air

With passage of the Air Carrier Access Act, U.S. airlines and terminals have become more accommodating. After the 1986 ruling, the Department of Transportation developed new regulations that outlaw discrimination against disabled travelers by describing the responsibilities of travelers, carriers, airport operators and contractors. For people with arthritis, the rules mean more time for boarding, accessible terminal parking and accessible restrooms, among other things.

Still, you must do your part. When you make airline reservations, always remember to state special needs, such as diet, seating or storage capacity for oversized arthritis aids. Allow extra time to get through the airport, request an airport wheelchair or other terminal transport if you need it and check your luggage through to your final destination.

To avoid security delays, make sure you haven't packed banned or questionable items in your carry-on bags. And be certain to have your photo ID and ticket at each checkpoint. If you have an artificial joint or metal shoe insert, you may undergo increased scrutiny. Consider carrying a medical alert card or note from your doctor.

Certain times of the day are less congested for airlines, making travel easier to negotiate. Reservationists also can recommend less crowded flights. If you must change planes, find out whether you also need to change terminals. If so, ask whether a shuttle between them is accessible. If not, ask for suggestions on making the move.

Traveling by train

Trains generally provide a good transportation option. Throughout Europe, rail travel is easy and accessible, with Eurostar trains accommodating disabled travelers on international routes. Keep in mind, however, that your foreign language skills may present challenges in getting exactly the help you need. In the United States, Amtrak offers special assistance and reduced fares for disabled passengers.

When making Amtrak reservations, ask for the special services desk. You can request accessible seating, assisted boarding and special meals. Most train stations have personnel to provide baggage assistance and to help passengers from the station entrance onto the train. If you have trouble walking, Amtrak can supply a wheelchair. Most stations have wheelchair lifts, but they request 24 hours' notice.

Range-of-motion exercises for travelers

You're on a long flight to London and feeling stiffer by the minute. Try these simple, in-your-seat exercises:

- Shoulder shrugs
- Ankle circles
- Head rolls
- Wrist rotators
- Praying hands
- Buns squeeze

To find out more about exercise, read *Arthritis: What Exercises Work*, by Dava Sobel and Arthur C. Klein, 1995; *Arthritis: Stop Suffering, Start Moving*, by Darlene Cohen, 1995; or *Exercise and Your Arthritis*, available from your local Arthritis Foundation office.

In addition, complementary redcap service is available at major stations. Be sure to get a claim for each bag you check. Understandably, Amtrak's plush trains are the most accommodating. All Superliner trains, for example, include accessible lower-level coach seating and two types of accessible sleeping accommodations.

Traveling by bus

Many bus lines have terminals with convenient restrooms, wide doorways and handrails. Most bus aisles, however, aren't wide enough for wheelchairs. If you use a wheelchair or have trouble using stairs, make arrangements with customer service for assistance in getting on and off the bus.

Because bus travel is often slower, you may want to schedule trips in midweek when fewer people travel. In addition, avoid trips with many transfers. Take along a pillow and nutritional snacks, such as fresh fruits, raw vegetables, no-salt crackers and peanut butter or low-fat cheese. Keep your medications and bottled water with you.

Traveling by car

When you travel by car, you'll enjoy more freedom than with any other form of transportation. You can stop whenever you want, you'll have more room to stretch out, and you can take along anything that will fit in your vehicle.

And there are ways to make the trip even more enjoyable. Be sure to stop as often as feasible, getting out to stretch and move around. Keep medications, snacks, maps, emergency kit and first-aid supplies in the car, and consider taking along a cellular phone. Your cell phone may not work overseas, but you can usually rent one at your destination. Make hotel or motel reservations in advance, or stop early enough to find a place to stay. Don't let yourself become overtired before finding a bed for the night.

When renting a car, ask for amenities that will make driving more comfortable, such as power steering, brakes and windows, cruise control, lift-up door handles, power side-view mirrors on both sides, and an easy-to-reach ignition. To get a car with these special features you may need to reserve your vehicle 4 to 6 weeks in advance.

Traveling by ship

You may find cruise travel particularly relaxing. Substantial design changes have been made to ships in recent years, such as widening their passageways, doorways and elevators, and accessible staterooms for wheelchair travelers have been added. Special diets and exercise plans may be available, too. Before booking with a particular cruise line, however, ask plenty of questions about the ship's design and accessibility. You'll want to book a cabin as close to the action as possible, but you'll need to decide if that means proximity to restaurants, pools or sun decks.

If you anticipate difficulty in embarking or disembarking, choose a cruise with fewer stops, or plan to stay on board soaking up the ship's ambience when others have gone ashore. Choices abound these days in cruises geared for the more leisurely traveler, and many shore excursions now accommodate those with an unhurried pace. Most ships employ doctors, but their pharmacies are limited. You'll want to take along more than enough medication to get you through the trip.

Touring overseas

Most countries have specific services designed for travelers who need special assistance. Whether you're touring Australia or Italy, Venezuela

Sister Gertrude's wheels

My three-wheeled Amigo, a battery-powered wheelchair, can't go more than 5 mph. But in France, a police officer pulled me over for speeding one September day.

I was on my way back to the hotel, after worshipping in Our Lady of Lourdes, a church built in a valley of the Pyrenees mountains to commemorate the Virgin Mary's appearance in 1858. Pilgrims go there for healing of body and soul. Rain pelted us as we left the church, and I was afraid that the water might damage my Amigo. So I was in a hurry to get back to the hotel, a half-mile away. But rolling along slowly in front of me was a long string of wheelchairs, perhaps 20 or more. So I pulled out into the road to pass them. That's when the police officer raised his hand and took out his ticket pad. He looked serious.

I guess I was supposed to follow the other wheelchairs without passing. Fortunately, some French-speaking lady in my travel group talked to the police officer. I don't know what she said, but it made him smile and he waved me on, without a ticket.

Months earlier, when I told my friends that I was going to Lourdes to fulfill a longtime dream, they said it was impossible. I was 73 years old. Damage from osteoarthritis had required me to have a knee replacement. I wore braces on my knees, back and neck. And I needed my Amigo to travel more than a few yards. But I found a tour company that specializes in trips for disabled people. And I got travel tips from many sources, such as the Arthritis Foundation, Mayo Clinic and the makers of my wheelchair.

On my Amigo I roamed airports and traveled the curb-cut streets of Lourdes, stopping at sidewalk cafes and, once, climbing a steep hill to a chapel. I even took a 3-day side trip to Paris on a 6-hour train ride through the beautiful countryside.

There were a few surprises, such as bus lifts that didn't always work. But I was determined to enjoy myself. And I did.

Sister Gertrude Ann
Rochester, Minn.

or Singapore, travel professionals are available to help make your trip easier. Many have brochures and Internet sites where you can find out more about what's offered in each country.

In addition, the International Association for Medical Assistance to Travelers offers a free information packet detailing its services, which include free climate and sanitation information and advice on international disease and immunization requirements. Travel Assistance International provides 24-hour medical referrals to travelers more than 100 miles from home.

Although health care has improved in many world destinations, be sure you're carrying ample medications on overseas trips and pace yourself so that you won't need a doctor to attend a routine flare-up or other short-term condition.

No matter where you're headed, whether it's New England or New Zealand, take all reasonable precautions to ensure your safety, health and well-being. Then relax and have fun. You can travel — and travel well — with arthritis.

Organizations that can help

Numerous travel agencies, tour operators, publications and other organizations can assist you in your quest to travel. Here is a sampling:

Accessible Journeys
35 W. Sellers Ave.
Ridley Park, PA 19078
610-521-0339
800-846-4537
www.disabilitytravel.com
Escorted group tours for slow walkers and wheelchair travelers

Cruise Planners
70 Garland Road
Nottingham, NH 03290
603-942-7191
800-801-9002
www.love2cruise.com
Specializes in cruise trips for passengers with disabilities

Discovery Hills Travel
886 Overlook Circle
San Marcos, CA 92078
760-744-6536
800-750-5975
www.discoveryhillstravel.com
Plans vacations for people with
special needs

Flying Wheels Travel
143 W. Bridge St.
P.O. Box 382
Owatonna, MN 55060
507-451-5005
www.flyingwheelstravel.com
Specializing in travel for people
with disabilities, with escorted
tours to international
destinations

**International Association for
Medical Assistance to Travelers**
417 Center St.
Lewiston, NY 14092
716-754-4883
www.iamat.org
Medical information and assistance for domestic and international travelers

Medical Travel
5184 Majorca Club Drive
Boca Raton, FL 33486
800-778-7953
www.medicaltravel.org
Provides planning for disabled
and special-needs travelers

New Mobility Magazine
603 Horsham Road
Horsham, PA 19044
215-675-9133
888-850-0344
www.newmobility.com
Magazine features articles on variety of topics of interest to people
with disabilities. Web site includes
travel links

**Society for Accessible Travel and
Hospitality**
347 Fifth Ave., Suite 610
New York, NY 10016
212-447-7284
www.sath.org
Provides information about
domestic and international transportation and lodging and names
of travel agents and tour operators
who specialize in arrangements for
disabled travelers

The Guided Tour
7900 Old York Road, Suite 114-B
Elkins Park, PA 19027
215-782-1370
800-783-5841
www.guidedtour.com
A professionally supervised vacation program in the United States
for people with developmental
and physical challenges

Travel Assistance International
9200 Keystone Crossing, Suite 300
Indianapolis, IN 46240
800-821-2828
www.travelassistance.com
Provides emergency evacuation
services and round-the-clock
medical referrals to travelers more
than 100 miles from home

Wilderness Inquiry
808 14th Ave. S.E.
Minneapolis, MN 55414
612-676-9400
800-728-0719
www.wildernessinquiry.org
Adventure travel for people of
all abilities

Finding help on the Web

- **Access-Able Travel Source**
  www.access-able.com
  Provides a database of services, stories and links for mature and
  disabled travelers, including accommodations and assistance in
  locating a travel agent.

- **Disability Travel and Recreation Resources**
  www.makoa.org/travel.htm
  A comprehensive collection of links to sites that include
  everything from tour companies to cruise lines.

- **Global Access**
  www.geocities.com/Paris/1502
  An online magazine with a list of disability travel links as well
  as informative tips and a resource guide for disabled travelers.

Chapter 12

On the job with arthritis

A rthritis is no reason to start planning an early retirement. With a positive attitude — focusing on what you can do instead of what you can't — you'll begin discovering creative solutions to the demands you face in the workplace. But your success at the job will depend greatly on having an upbeat attitude, a strong belief that you can and will get on with your life.

One of the first challenges you face is whether to tell your boss and your co-workers about your arthritis. Many people are afraid to do this. And with good reason. In some cases arthritis raises questions in your employer's mind about whether you're physically able to do the job. Some who don't understand that arthritis is more than just aches and pains may also wonder whether you're using the disease as an excuse for special treatment. And in some job situations, unspoken discrimination will show up as denied opportunities, such as promotions you earn and deserve but don't get.

For reasons such as these, many experts recommend that you say nothing about the disease if you can answer no to the following questions:

• Is your arthritis obvious?
• Do you need special accommodations or resources to do the job?

If, however, you answer yes to one of these questions, it's usually best to tell your employer and co-workers that you have arthritis.

Otherwise, they may grow to believe you aren't carrying your share of the load — and they may resent you for it. If you say nothing and try to keep the arthritis a secret, you'll probably try to overcome the hard feelings of your colleagues by ignoring your body's warning signs and pushing yourself beyond your limits. This will only make matters worse by increasing the pain and fatigue so common to arthritis.

If you decide you need to tell your boss about the disease, schedule a meeting with care. Pick a time of the day and week when distractions and job pressures for both of you are lower than usual. Then explain that you have arthritis. Give your boss a short course about the disease. If you have rheumatoid arthritis, you might explain that when the pain flares up or fatigue sets in, these are signs that the tissues around your affected joints need rest and repair.

Go into this meeting with suggestions about changes that will help you do a better job. You'll need to do a little research to come up with these ideas. Talk with your doctor or an occupational therapist about your work responsibilities. They'll have ideas to help you perform certain tasks more easily, perhaps with the aid of assistive devices — such as armrests on your chair — or with exercises that will increase your dexterity and range of motion for any repeated movements you'll have to do. (At the end of this chapter you'll find a list of organizations that help with job-accommodation ideas and assistive devices.)

Know your rights

Read up on the Americans With Disabilities Act passed by Congress in 1990. It's the most extensive bill of rights for people with disabilities ever signed into law. Your arthritis may be a disability under the law.

This law bans discrimination against people with disabilities, and it requires companies with more than 15 employees to make reasonable changes that will help you do your job. In fact, wise employers will value your experience and will be willing to give you the tools necessary for you to do your job well. Among the possible reasonable accommodations are the following:

- Providing or modifying equipment to help you perform your job tasks, such as a wheeled cart to carry supplies, a headphone instead of a hand-held receiver or a chair with good back support. The cost of some assistive devices may qualify your employer for tax benefits.

- Providing a ramp if you have difficulty with stairs. If accommodations or special equipment is required, the employer cannot make you pay for it. An exception would be if the changes place an undue hardship on the employer, causing significant expense or difficulty. What constitutes undue hardship is a matter judged on a case-by-case basis.
- Adjusting the height of your desk.
- Allowing break periods for rest.
- Changing your job responsibilities, eliminating tasks you can't perform that are not essential to your job.

If you believe your employer treats you unfairly and is unwilling to make reasonable changes to help you do your job, you can file a formal complaint with the Equal Employment Opportunity Commission (EEOC). Free brochures about the Americans With Disabilities Act are available from the EEOC (information about obtaining these is at the end of this chapter). Your state also may have laws to protect you from discrimination. If you have questions about your legal rights, you may also wish to speak with a lawyer who specializes in employment law.

Protect your joints

Finding ways to reduce or eliminate activities that inflame and damage your joints can keep you off disability and in the workforce longer. Here are some suggestions:

- Arrange your office or work area to reduce the amount of lifting, walking or other movement that may be painful.
- Find the most comfortable position for doing your work.
- If you perform repetitive motions, such as typing or assembly work, rest the affected joints every 20 to 30 minutes by stretching your muscles. In fact, even if you don't perform repetitive motions, try to take a short break every half-hour or hour. Change positions, stretch and relax for a minute or two.
- If one particular task is always painful, search for other ways to do it. Occupational therapists specialize in solving such problems. Another option might be to ask a co-worker to help you out in exchange for your help on something else.
- Use special tools or assistive devices that reduce strain on your joints: electric staplers, dictation services, chair-leg extensions (to make it easier to get up) and enlarged grips for pencils and pens.

Exercise

Maintaining the muscle strength around your joints helps keep the joints stable and more comfortable. Your doctor and your physical therapist can design an exercise program that allows you to work on the joints that you use most often in your job. Some of the exercises can be simple and inconspicuous enough that you can do them at lunch or during momentary breaks. For example, if you work a lot with your hands, you can take a few seconds to bend your fingers, wrists and elbows as far as you can, then stretch them back out.

Relax

In a tortuous cycle, job stress can aggravate arthritic pain, which intensifies the job stress. One way to break this cycle is to learn relaxation techniques. Following are a few ideas:
- Let your mind wander to a happy memory.
- Look out a window and study a pleasant scene.
- Listen to music or a tape of relaxing sounds, such as the ocean surf or a gentle rain.
- Sit outside or take a short walk.
- Lie down or sit quietly for a few minutes and, with eyes closed, practice deep breathing. Then, starting with your toes, tighten the muscles and then release them. Work your way up to your scalp, then let your mind and body slip into a minute of relaxation. Don't do this, however, if tensing your muscles aggravates your arthritis.

Conserve your energy

Arthritis can cause fatigue. You can help avoid fatigue by pacing yourself and by doing the most important projects during your time of peak energy. For example, if you're a morning person and you do various tasks throughout the day, spend the morning doing the work that requires the most concentration and energy. In addition, schedule working breathers by alternating difficult tasks with easier ones. If possible, take a rest break of about 10 minutes every few hours.

Be a smarter commuter

For some with arthritis, the trip to work can become a painful and exhausting gauntlet of obstacles: stress-inducing traffic, driving a vehicle that isn't equipped for people with restricted movement, then walking from the company's distant parking lot and up a flight of stairs. Each one of these can cause a flare-up of arthritic pain and can sap your energy before the workday begins. Try these ideas:

- Share a ride with someone who works with you or in your area. Pay for the service or take turns driving.
- Use public transportation. It's usually slower but is less exhausting than driving in bumper-to-bumper traffic. All public transportation has to be accessible to people with disabilities, according to the Americans With Disabilities Act.
- If you must drive, install equipment that will minimize the discomfort: backrest, special mirrors, steering wheel modifications. Some automakers give you rebates when you install these kinds of equipment in new cars, and they'll give you a list of companies in your area that will do the installation.
- If you have trouble walking, ask your employer for a parking space near the entrance. You can get a parking decal for the disabled by contacting your state transportation department. This permits you to use parking spaces reserved for the handicapped.
- If you have difficulty with stairs, you may need to ask for a ramp leading into the building. You might also request a work space near the entrance.

Make friends with your computer

Working at a keyboard for the better part of 8 hours a day can worsen the pain and fatigue of arthritis.

If you find yourself at the computer for hours on end, consider these tips:

- As you sit in your chair, lean back slightly so that your lower back is against the backrest. Keep your feet flat on the floor, with your knees bent at about 90 degrees or slightly more. If you have no firm lumbar support in this position, ask for a chair that allows you to adjust the backrest to different heights and angles.
- Scoot up close to the keyboard, so you aren't reaching out at it. The keyboard should be about 3 to 6 inches from your lap. Both the keyboard and the monitor should be directly in front of you. The top of the monitor screen should be at eye level. Otherwise, you'll need to bend your neck uncomfortably up or down to see the screen.

- A wrist rest, or padded bar, between the keyboard and your lap provides wrist support by giving your hands a place to rest as you type. While typing, your wrists should be straight, with your forearms parallel to the floor. Wrist braces can help keep your wrists in the proper position. And chairs with armrests offer support for the forearms. If your wrists are usually bent as you type and have no support, you can develop carpal tunnel syndrome. This produces pain or numbness in your hand, which can radiate to your arm. In most cases an operation is needed to correct this problem.
- If typing is hard for you, use a mouse as much as possible. Another option is voice-activation software. This allows you to dictate to the computer, which types the words as you speak. Early editions of this software, running on computers slower than we have now, required you to speak each word slowly and distinctly. But as software improved and computer speeds increased, the pace of dictation sped up as well. You can now dictate without pausing between words.
- Take short breaks from the computer to stretch your legs, arms and fingers. Give your eyes a break by focusing on something at a distance, such as an object out the window or across the room.

Keep an open mind about your job and career

Despite all that you and your employer can do to accommodate for your arthritis, the nature of your job or the progression of your arthritis may require you to cut back on the number of hours you work or to find another line of work.

If your job requires heavy physical labor, such as construction, your doctor may refer you to an occupational therapist or to a vocational rehabilitation agency to build your strength and to determine how much weight you can safely lift. If the restrictions are such that there's no job you can do in the company, the vocational rehabilitation agency will help you find a job that you can do. Sometimes, workers decide to join the ranks of a related company. A construction worker, for example, may join an organization that makes equipment for the construction industry.

The chair

When I accepted an editor's job at a religious organization, I inherited an overstuffed chair built decades before "lumbar support" became a golden phrase among advertisers in spiffy suits.

To edit at my computer, I had to scoot forward. This left my spine with no support but thin air. Within a couple of years, my lower back developed a grinding, relentless ache so persistent that it felt like an alien parasite with spurs had strapped itself onto my spine to play ride 'em cowboy.

My family physician took X-rays of my spine, saw nothing unusual and prescribed back-strengthening exercises. Months later, the pain had not lessened. So I went to an orthopedic surgeon, X-rays in tow. He immediately noticed degenerated cartilage between some of the lower disks, and he diagnosed osteoarthritis. He said I was suffering partly because I lived a sedentary lifestyle, working as an editor. (I wonder if I should have told him I had two kids younger than 5.) The doc gave me new exercises and suggested I walk 2 miles a day.

I called my lunchtime treks around the organizational complex "once around Jericho." Not a brick on the facility ever trembled in the slightest, but I felt as though my spine was crumbling.

As the words "lumbar" and "ergonomic" began making headlines, I thought about asking for a new chair. But when I saw the price tag, I couldn't muster the courage — I worked for a nonprofit organization. And the chair might not help. But when the pain subsided during a long vacation, I decided to ask for the chair as soon as I got back. Wouldn't you know it, during the vacation my editorial assistant had my ancient chair reupholstered.

So I kept the chair — and my back pain — for the duration. Several years later I left the job to start a freelance editorial service. I bought a spine-friendly chair that has so many adjustments that I could dance with it. And after a few months I felt like dancing, because my back pain was gone.

Stephen
Kansas City, Mo.

Finding a new job

Take a personal inventory

The search for a new job doesn't start in the classified ads, in the office of a career counselor or at the family computer, updating your resume. The search begins within, as you take stock of your resources, realistically but positively: physical ability, educational background, job experience and personality are all things to consider.

It's important to identify the kinds of jobs you're able to do. But it's just as important to identify the kinds of jobs you want to do. To discover what these are, many career counselors advise that you begin by thinking about your values. Do you want to help people and leave the world a better place? Are you a self-motivated worker who loves independence? Do you value job security? Do you want to be an expert in your field? Do you crave recognition?

Honest answers to questions like these will help you sort through the job opportunities ahead. The answers may also prod you to get training in another field that interests you.

Find job openings

Don't lean heavily on the classified ads. Competition for the jobs listed there is often fierce because many job hunters haven't learned the more effective techniques for tracking down a good job. Besides, some ads are for jobs that don't exist. Job listings with post office box numbers are sometimes from placement services trying to build a stable of job seekers so that they'll have names ready when companies come looking for applicants.

One of the best ways to get a job — often before it's advertised — is to draw on your network of contacts: family, friends, former employers and co-workers, instructors and fellow students at seminars, members of associations to which you belong, professionals you know (physicians, accountants), even casual acquaintances. Don't be shy about describing the kind of job you're seeking and why you're excited about the potential.

Some other ideas for finding job openings are listed here:

- Expand your network. Join a civic organization. Join a national association in your chosen field and attend workshops at its convention. Take a community college course on the subject and meet others interested in the same career.
- Call companies that have people doing the kind of work that interests you. Ask to speak to one of those employees. Tell the person that you're thinking of entering the field and that you'd like to

make an appointment to talk for 10 minutes to find out what the job is like. This conversation gives you insight into the job and the company, and it may open the door to employment.

- Many large companies have Web sites or job lines with recorded messages identifying current openings.
- Job fairs have become increasingly popular for both employers and job hunters, especially in large cities. Get a list of employers who will attend, choose several that capture your interest, then research them. This way, you'll have an educated response to the recruiter's question about why you want to work there. Get the recruiter's business card and follow up with a letter and a phone call.
- You can attend "virtual" job fairs on the Web if you have access to a personal computer and the Internet.
- Read the classified ads in the newspaper, on the Internet and in trade journals.
- Contact the career services or job placement office of the institution from which you graduated and have it place your resume in its databank. Some schools have special placement services for alumni in transition.
- Contact state and federal employment centers. Some local Arthritis Foundations also have a job placement service.

Update your resume

On one page, briefly outline your career goal, qualifications, experience and education. Make no mention of your health. Use easily readable type on light paper, such as white or ivory. Colored paper can be hard to photocopy.

If you're answering an ad that has specific terminology, such as the name of a computer software that you need to know, use the terms if you have the requested expertise. Some companies hire screeners to review resumes, searching for those terms.

Don't use a generic resume for all of your job queries. Adapt your resume, highlighting facts pertinent to the individual company.

Some companies use resume-scanning technology to convert paper documents to digital format. Follow their instructions to make sure your resume is scannable.

Write a cover letter

A cover letter personalizes your resume or job application form, introducing you to the employer. So if at all possible, address it to a person.

If you're responding to an ad that mentions no one by name, call the company and ask who does the hiring.

The letter should contain about three paragraphs. The opening should specify the job you want and the reason you're applying. If someone in the company suggested you apply, mention his or her name. In the second paragraph, explain why you want to work for this company. Identify your top qualifications for the job, but avoid sweeping statements such as, "I'm a hard worker." Close the letter in the third paragraph by promising to call the employer for a meeting and by thanking the person for considering you.

Keep the neatly typed letter to one page. And if possible, match the typeface and the high-quality paper used on your resume. Carefully proofread the letter, then ask someone else to review it. A single misspelling could send an unintended, even disqualifying message. Sign the letter in blue or black ink.

Complete the application

Some employers say that the way you fill out a job application reveals as much about you as the answers you give. If the completed application is sloppy and unorganized, the employer may conclude that your job performance will be just as shoddy. But if the application is filled out neatly and in the manner requested, the employer's first impression will be that you have the potential to become a conscientious worker who follows directions.

Read the entire application before filling it out. Otherwise, you might begin writing in cursive, only to discover a request to print. Or you might use a pencil, and find out later that you should've used a pen. Pen is usually preferred because pencil doesn't always photocopy well. Neatness is so important on the application that if you make a mistake, get a fresh copy and start over.

Have on hand all of the information you need to complete the application: names, addresses and phone numbers of your references, schools you attended and the dates you graduated, a list of your previous jobs, the years you worked there, and the names and phone numbers of your bosses. Don't simply fill in these spaces with "See resume." Most employers prefer storing all of the necessary information on one convenient form: their tailored application.

Don't write in a dollar amount when asked about the salary you want. Shooting too high will show that you don't know what the going rate of pay is in your field. Shooting too low will make employers wonder why you don't think you're worth more. Consider putting in "open to discussion," a friendlier response than "negotiable."

Employers aren't supposed to ask questions about your age, race, religion and family. You may leave the responses to such questions blank.

Though employers aren't allowed to ask if you have a disability, they may ask if you're able to perform the job functions. A sample question might be: "Do you have any physical limitations that would hinder your performance in the job for which you're applying?" Questions such as this put you in an awkward situation if you think you'll need some kind of assistance in doing the work. Some career counselors say that at this early stage in the job hunt don't disclose that you have arthritis. They argue that doing so could eliminate you as a candidate without giving you a chance to discuss the matter. For this reason, they suggest answering no, under the presumption that the employer will provide the legally required reasonable accommodations if this becomes necessary. Another possible response if you're not sure how your arthritis will affect your job performance is to write: "Will discuss."

Prepare for the interview

If your arthritis will be obvious to the interviewer, consider dropping a hint about it during the phone conversation — but only after you make the interview appointment, and only if the person you're talking to is the one who will be interviewing you. Possible hint: "I sometimes have trouble with stairs. Do you have an elevator?" Hints like this may help reduce the shock, making it easier for the interviewer to concentrate on your discussion.

Compile a list of questions often asked in an interview, then compose and rehearse your answers. (You'll find sample questions in the job-hunting books and Internet career sites listed at the end of this chapter.) Approach the interview as a performance because you are on stage and you are being carefully reviewed. Dress for the part, present yourself as positive and enthusiastic and know your lines. This is not improvisational theater.

Perhaps the most popular interview question is this: "Tell me about yourself."

Don't think of this as a pleasant icebreaker. It could be the most dangerous question of the day for you — or the most beneficial. Law prohibits employers from basing their hiring decisions on age, sex, race, religion, health or nonfelony arrests. They aren't supposed to ask, "How's your health?" But in describing yourself, you may reveal the answer. If you plan, however, you can answer the question well and avoid revealing the "illegal" information, unless you want to do so.

Briefly summarize assets you would bring to the job. For example, you could say that you placed a high value on education, earned a college degree in your chosen career and were fortunate enough to have had two excellent jobs in the field. You could add that your experience, your desire to excel and your eagerness to accept new challenges have led you here.

If your arthritis is obvious, you may want to mention it briefly. But don't shift the focus to your limitations. Talk about adjustments you've made that allow you to stay productive. For instance, you could say something like this: "Since walking isn't my strong point, I've learned to organize and plan carefully to save steps." Or a broader approach: "I know you're legally prohibited from asking about my arthritis, except questions about how I would do specific tasks required on the job. But I'd be happy to answer any questions you have because I'm certain I can do the work."

If your arthritis isn't obvious but will require job accommodations, you face a tough dilemma that has no easy solution. Should you say nothing until you have a job offer? If so, you can be certain that you won't be ruled out because of your disability. But the employer might feel misled. And this could generate hard feelings and a shaky start to your new job. Another approach is to tell the employer about your arthritis, especially if you know there are areas in which you'll need some accommodation very soon. Employers aren't obligated to provide accommodations until you tell them that you have a disability. If you decide this is the best solution for you, mention that the accommodations are usually inexpensive and well worth the investment.

After the interview, send a short letter of appreciation. Thank the interviewer for talking with you. Then mention something about the interview to refresh the person's memory, repeat your interest in the job and express your desire to hear from the company.

With a positive outlook and thoughtful preparation, you have every right to be hopeful about your future in the workplace.

Organizations that can help

Job hunting

What Color Is Your Parachute? This is a career handbook that author Richard N. Bolles has updated each year for more than three decades. It's full of time-tested strategies for changing jobs.

Successful Job Search Strategies for the Disabled: Understanding the ADA. This is a comprehensive career guide written by Jeffrey G. Allen, a certified placement counselor who is also an employment attorney.

The Internet has many career sites. These offer information on testing, counseling and job listings. Here is a sampling:

America's Job Bank
www.ajb.dni.us

Career Action Center
www.careeraction.org

CareerBuilder
www.careerbuilder.com

Monster.com
www.monster.com

monsterTRAK
www.jobtrak.com

USAJOBS
a listing of government jobs
www.usajobs.opm.gov

U.S. Small Business Administration
www.sbaonline.sba.gov

The National Board for Certified Counselors, free of charge, will identify certified career counselors in your area. Call 800-398-5389.

Your local Arthritis Foundation may have job placement services. They also offer the free brochure *Arthritis in the Workplace*.

National headquarters:

Arthritis Foundation
P.O. Box 7669
Atlanta, GA 30357
800-283-7800
www.arthritis.org

Assistive devices

ABLEDATA, A National Database of Assistive Technology Information
8630 Fenton St., Suite 930
Silver Spring, MD 20910
800-227-0216
www.abledata.com

Job Accommodation Network
West Virginia University
918 Chestnut Ridge Road, Suite 1
P.O. Box 6080
Morgantown, WV 26506
800-526-7234
www.jan.wvu.edu

Office of Disability Employment Policy (ODEP)
1331 F St. N.W., Suite 300
Washington, DC 20004
202-376-6200
www.dol.gov/dol/odep

National Rehabilitation Information Center
4200 Forbes Boulevard, Suite 202
Lanham, MD 20706
800-346-2742
www.naric.com

American Occupational Therapy Association
4720 Montgomery Lane
P.O. Box 31220
Bethesda, MD 20824-1220
301-652-2682
www.aota.org

Legal issues

U.S. Equal Employment Opportunity Commission
1801 L St. N.W.
Washington, DC 20507
202-663-4900
800-669-4000
www.eeoc.gov
Free brochures: *The Americans With Disabilities Act: Questions and Answers* and *The Americans With Disabilities Act: Your Employment Rights as an Individual With a Disability* (available online)

Americans With Disabilities Act
800-514-0301
Information line, answers questions:

Department of Justice
Civil Rights Division
950 Pennsylvania Ave. N.W.
Washington, DC 20530
800-514-0301
www.usdoj.gov/crt

American Bar Association
541 N. Fairbanks Ct.
Chicago, IL 60611
800-285-2221
www.abanet.org

Chapter 13

Where to get more help

One book can't provide everything you'd like to know about arthritis. Fortunately, reliable information is readily available. Here are selected sources, plus some general recommendations on how to search for health information.

The Arthritis Foundation

The Arthritis Foundation is an excellent source of information and support. This national organization works mainly through state and regional chapters. It offers self-help materials, support groups, exercise and water aerobics classes and lists of doctors in your area who are experienced in working with people who have arthritis. Primary funding comes from contributions, bequests and grants from the United Way and other organizations.

The business white pages of the telephone book lists local Arthritis Foundation chapters. To order informational brochures, subscribe to the magazine *Arthritis Today* or learn how to contact your local chapter, call the Arthritis Foundation at 800-283-7800. The Arthritis Foundation's address is P.O. Box 7669, Atlanta, GA 30357. The telephone number of the national office is 404-872-7100. Many countries outside the United

States — including Canada, Australia and New Zealand — have similar organizations. The telephone number of the national office of the Canadian Arthritis Society is 416-979-7228.

Mayo Clinic health information

Mayo Clinic offers numerous resources for reliable health information. Mayo Clinic's Health Information Web site at *www.MayoClinic.com* provides timely, accurate information on many health topics, including arthritis. To access information on arthritis from the home page, click Conditions Center and then click Arthritis.

From time to time, the monthly publications *Mayo Clinic Health Letter* and *Mayo Clinic Women's HealthSource* contain information about recent developments in arthritis treatment. Get subscription information by calling 800-333-9037.

Surfing the Web

If you have a personal computer and Internet access, you can find a lot of information on the Web. The Food and Drug Administration (FDA) and many other government agencies, private organizations, groups and individuals use the Web to offer in-depth information. Here are some of the better Web sites for locating reliable information about arthritis:
- The Arthritis Foundation Web site at *www.arthritis.org*.
- The Department of Health and Human Services Web site at *www.healthfinder.gov*. The site offers links to the Web sites of clearinghouses, databases, support groups and government agencies. Go to the home page, click Health Library and select Diseases and Conditions. You'll find an alphabetical list that includes arthritis.

Use government information on the Web to compare the benefits of managed care health insurance plans offered in your area. A government Medicare site provides comparative information at *www.medicare.gov/ mphCompare/home.asp*. Search this information by state or Zip code. View benefits for a single plan or directly compare the benefits of two separate plans.
- The National Institute of Arthritis and Musculoskeletal and Skin Diseases (NIAMS), part of the National Institutes of Health, at *www.niams.nih.gov/hi*.

- The American Medical Association and several other medical associations have a Web site that includes information on health conditions. To access arthritis information, go to *www.medem.com*, click Library Entry, and in the Diseases and Conditions section, click Bone, Joint and Rheumatic Conditions.
- The American College of Rheumatology at *www.rheumatology.org*. You can access arthritis information and the latest press releases from the home page.

Be specific when searching on the Web

Sometimes it's difficult to know just which search terms to use. Say you want to find out how much fat you should have in your diet. Do you search under *diet, nutrition, fat,* or *low-fat?* One approach is to start with directory sites that list popular search terms and topics for you.

Your search will evolve as you get deeper into a subject. As you begin reading about a particular health topic, look for additional words or phrases under which to search. You may want to search using both lay and medical terms for a condition or disease. Use a medical dictionary to help you. For example, if you're looking for information on arthritis, you may also want to search under the medical term *rheumatic diseases.* As you read information online, also note the names of experts and health-related organizations that are mentioned. Then you may want to search under those names.

If you get too many results the first time you do a search, try using qualifier words, such as *and, or* and *not* to help limit your search. For example, try *arthritis and treatments.* Most sites that have search functions offer search tips on their home page.

Reminder: Don't let the Web replace traditional health care. The health information you glean from the Web can make you a better informed consumer when talking with your doctor. But remember that health information intended for a wide audience can't be a substitute for the personalized care and advice you receive from your physician. Health information is a place to start — not an end in itself.

Your local library

Become familiar with the resources available at your public library. Reference areas routinely stock medical dictionaries, and the periodical section may carry the monthly *Arthritis Today.* Find out which books about arthritis are on the shelves. If you're considering purchasing costly equipment, check the consumer information section. Today's technology makes libraries the source of information from around the world. Ask the reference librarian about the best way to search for information you need. If you don't own a computer, your library may have one you can use at no charge. The reference librarian can also explain whether, and how, you can use your home computer to search through the library's card catalog.

Most local libraries also are linked to other library systems. Although your library may not subscribe to medical journals, for example, it may have computer access to health periodical indices. Some libraries will fax articles to you, or you can request an interlibrary loan. If you live near a medical school or large medical center, the library resources there may be available to you. You will find specialized journals that public libraries don't carry.

Bookstores

If you're looking for a recent or specific publication that your library may not have, visit a large bookstore. Consider books endorsed by the Arthritis Foundation. A highly regarded resource is *Arthritis: A Take Care of Yourself Health Guide*, Fifth Edition, by James F. Fries, M.D., 1999. A book which emphasizes proper nutrition and exercise as ways to stay healthy and active with arthritis is *Strong Women and Men Beat Arthritis*, by Miriam E. Nelson, Ph.D., 2002.

Words of caution

Be careful where you get health information. It seems that every time you open a newspaper, turn on the TV or read a magazine, you find contradictory or confusing health information. Medical misinformation is not new, but it has proliferated since the introduction of the World Wide Web. It's generally accepted that there are more than 100,000 health-related Web sites, and a Harris Poll taken in 2001 found that nearly 100 million Americans go online for health information.

The Web is a source of seemingly endless medical information, some of it very good, but some of it downright bad medical advice. Don't believe everything you read on the Web. Anyone who has the necessary

Buyer beware

Each year one of every four Americans use quack medical treatments, spending a total of at least $27 billion for these treatments. At best, the drugs, devices and lifestyle changes are worthless. At worst, they may lead to physical harm and even death. Medical quackery succeeds because people yearn for a quick cure.

The American Medical Association estimates that most victims of fraudulent medical treatments spend $500 to $1,000 annually. But beyond being useless and expensive, sometimes fraudulent medical treatments are actually dangerous. Medications, even vitamins, that are harmless when taken in moderation may be very dangerous when taken in doses prescribed by the quack.

Watch out for promotions that describe medical treatments with adjectives such as *secret, proven, miracle, foreign, breakthrough* and *overnight.* Also be wary of glowing testimonials from happy patients. Quacks tend to claim they're fighting against a conspiracy of established physicians who are unwilling to acknowledge new treatments. They claim their products provide a complete cure without any side effects. And they often exert pressure, claiming that this is a "limited offer," available for only a short time. At this time, there is no cure for arthritis. But there are many ways to have a positive impact on your health.

hardware and software can publish a health information Web page or offer medical advice in an online chat forum. And the Internet has a way of making all health information appear equal. Be particularly wary of products offered for sale online.

Stick with reliable sources for your medical advice. Before you delve too far into a radical new treatment, whether on the Web or elsewhere, determine who's sponsoring it. Is the sponsor qualified to give medical advice or sell something? Is the information updated frequently? Is it reviewed by health care professionals? Ask whether newspaper or magazine articles attribute the information to a respected publication, organization or medical professional. Carefully examine statistics. It typically takes years of consecutive studies to prove cause and effect. Read reports about medical studies carefully and check sources. Did the study involve a large number of people? Was there a control group? Do the results show a cause-and-effect relationship or an association between two factors? Has the work been published in a peer-reviewed medical journal? If something you find sounds questionable or conflicts with conventional wisdom, be skeptical. If health news makes you question your treatment, medication or diet, ask your doctor whether the information applies to you.

Glossary

acupuncture. The practice of piercing specific sites on the body, called pathways or meridians, with thin needles in an attempt to relieve pain associated with some chronic disorders.

anesthesiologist. A doctor who is often involved in treating the pain of arthritis through the use of nerve blocks.

angiography. The X-ray depiction of blood vessels following introduction of contrast material into the bloodstream. Used as a tool to diagnose diseases that affect the blood vessels, including inflammatory diseases.

antibody. A globulin protein produced by the blood that selectively reacts with the protein (antigen) that stimulated its development. In autoimmune disease, antibodies may react with the body's own tissues.

antigen. Any substance capable of inducing an immune response resulting in production of a specific antibody or sensitized lymphocyte that interacts with the antigen. In some autoimmune and arthritic diseases, the body's own tissues may act as antigens.

antinuclear antibodies. The antibodies that interact with cell nuclei. Commonly found in certain autoimmune diseases, including arthritis.

arthrocentesis. A procedure using a needle to puncture and withdraw (aspirate) fluid from a joint for medical tests to help with diagnosis. May also be used to inject medication into a joint.

arthroplasty. Joint surgery done to improve function. May involve insertion of metal alloy or high-density plastic materials or total joint replacement.

arthroscopy. An examination of the interior of a joint with a small camera mounted in the tip of a tube that's inserted into the joint through a small incision in the skin. The instrument is called an arthroscope.

autoimmune disease. A condition in which the body's immune system reacts against its own tissues. This process is thought to occur in rheumatoid arthritis and some related diseases.

biopsy. The removal of a sample of body tissue for examination — usually microscopic — to aid in diagnosis. A biopsy of a joint may help diagnose an unusual form of arthritis.

bursa. A sac or sac-like cavity filled with synovial fluid and situated to reduce friction between body tissues.

cartilage. A fibrous connective tissue. Found in the lining of joints and in the flexible portions of the nose and the ears.

collagen. A long protein fiber that connects and strengthens various tissues.

complement system. A complex series of proteins that interact with antigen-antibody complexes that are involved in immune and inflammatory reactions. Complement reactions occur in rheumatoid arthritis and lupus erythematosus.

computed tomography (CT). A method of displaying cross-sections of the body, including joints and the spine, that uses a sequential series of X-rays.

cyclooxygenases (COX). These enzymes are involved in the production of prostaglandins, hormone-like substances that trigger inflammation. COX-1 is involved in maintaining normal body functions. COX-2 is more involved in inflammatory reactions.

cyst. A closed cavity or sac in the body.

cytokines. Proteins released by cells that direct cell actions. There are numerous types and sources of cytokines. Similar substances are named lymphokines and interleukins and are prominently involved in inflammation.

elastin. A type of connective fiber which is flexible and elastic in various tissues. Helps hold tissues in place.

endothelium. A layer of cells that lines cavities of the body, such as inside joints.

enthesis. The site of attachment of muscle or ligament to bone.

epidemiology. The study of the causes of diseases, such as arthritis, by determining their frequencies and relationships to events in the environment.

frozen shoulder. A painful limitation of motion of the shoulder resulting from chronic inflammation of the rotator cuff.

glucocorticoids. Hormones released from the adrenal glands that affect carbohydrate metabolism. Examples include cortisone and prednisone, which have powerful anti-inflammatory actions but also adverse side effects.

Heberden's nodes. Small, bony nodules found in the fingertip (distal) joints in osteoarthritis.

human leukocyte antigens (HLA). Proteins that influence the body's immune system function. Certain types are associated with diseases such as rheumatoid arthritis.

hyaluronic acid. A protein found in large amounts in synovial fluid of joints. It may be altered in arthritis. *See* synovial fluid.

immune complex. The combination of an antigen and antibody. Immune complexes may interact with proteins such as the complement system and produce inflammation and tissue injury. *See* complement system.

immune system. The cells and tissues that protect the body against infection. Disordered immune system function has been associated with the development of arthritis and other diseases.

immunoglobulins. Also known as antibodies and gamma globulins, they're induced by and released in the blood after infections, immunizations and some arthritic diseases, such as lupus erythematosus.

joint. The junction between two or more bones. The most common is the synovial joint, which permits relatively free movement and is most often affected by arthritis. Synovial joints contain a synovial membrane lining on the inside of the joint, which produces nutrients and lubricants for the joint. *See* synovial fluid and synovial membrane.

laminectomy. The surgical removal of part of a vertebra. Usually done to relieve pressure on a spinal nerve caused by a herniated disk or bony spur.

leukocytes. White blood cells. Found in blood, lymphocytes and bone marrow, they accumulate in areas of inflammation.

ligament. A band of fibrous tissue that connects bones or cartilages. For example, ligaments that cross joints give strength and stability to those joints.

lymphocyte. A type of white blood cell involved in immune reactions of the body in most inflammatory and autoimmune diseases.

magnetic resonance imaging (MRI). A method of imaging tissues of the body using powerful magnets. Cross-sections of soft tissues as well as bone can be depicted.

myopathy. Any disease involving muscle. Polymyositis is an example of an inflammatory myopathy that results in muscle weakness.

neuropathy. Any disease involving nerves. One or more large nerves may be affected (mononeuropathy) or many small peripheral nerves (polyneuropathy).

occupational therapist. A professional trained to help maximize physical potential at home and in the workplace through use of assistive devices and lifestyle adaptations.

osteomyelitis. An infection of bone.

osteoporosis. Abnormally reduced bone density. May predispose a person to fractures after slight trauma.

physiatrist. A doctor who specializes in physical medicine and rehabilitation. A physiatrist evaluates and recommends treatments that restore function in people with chronic disease.

physical therapist. A trained professional who teaches exercises and other physical activities to aid in rehabilitation and maximize physical ability with less pain.

reflex sympathetic dystrophy. A condition involving the hand or foot and characterized by pain, swelling, coldness and sweating. Also called complex regional pain syndrome.

rheumatic fever. An acute disease involving joints, skin, the heart and other tissues, usually occurring in children, and caused by the body's reaction to a preceding streptococcal infection.

rheumatologist. A doctor who specializes in the diagnosis and treatment of musculoskeletal disorders, including arthritis.

rotator cuff. The tendons of the shoulder muscles that form a sleeve-like structure around the joint. Pain and tenderness from injury or inflammation is referred to as rotator cuff syndrome.

syndesmophytes. A bony outgrowth from a ligament. May be tender when forming and block normal joint movement.

synovectomy. The removal of a synovial membrane from inside a joint such as the knee. May be performed to treat diseases such as rheumatoid arthritis.

synovial fluid. A fluid that lubricates joint surfaces during movement and supplies the joint cartilages with nutrients. Normally, it is viscous and transparent, but with inflammation, it becomes turbid and watery and contains white blood cells.

synovial membrane. The inner lining of synovial joints. *See* joint.

tendon. A fibrous cord by which a muscle is attached to a bone or another structure.

tophus. A chalky deposit of urate occurring in gout. Tophi form most often around joints but may occur in other areas such as ear cartilage.

Index

Note: Glossary definitions are indicated by the **boldface** page numbers.

A

Acupuncture, 136–137, **185**
Adrenal crisis, 97
Aerobic exercise, 29–30, 36–37, 50
Air travel, 157, 158
Alternative medicine, 135–146
Americans With Disabilities Act, 166–167
Analgesics, 88, 110, 111–112, 119
Anesthesiologists, **185**
Angiogenesis, 148
Angiography, **185**
Ankle surgery, 131
Ankylosing spondylitis, 12
Anti-inflammatory drugs, 86–98, 115–116
Anti-TNF medications, 108–110, 148
Antibiotics and arthritis, 149
Antibody, **185**
Anticoagulants and NSAIDs, 90
Antidepressant drugs, 113
Antigen, **185**
Antinuclear antibodies, **185**
Antioxidants, 142, 152
Aromatherapy, 137
Arthritis
  causes and effects, 2
  common forms, 4–14
  promising research, 147–152
Arthritis Foundation, 84, 179–180
Arthrocentesis, **185**
Arthrodesis. *See* Joint fusion
Arthroplasty, 123, 125–131, **186**
Arthroscopic debridement, 122
Arthroscopy, **186**
Aspirin, 87–88, 111, 115
Assistive devices, 22–28, 167, 178
Autoimmune disease, 92, 102, **186**

Autologous transfusion, 132
Avocado oil, 142–143

B

Back exercises, 47
Bee venom therapy, 137–138
Behavior therapy for pain, 57
Ben-Gay, 112
Biofeedback, 57, 138
Biologic agents, 108–111
Biopsy, **186**
Blood filtering, 109
Bone resection, 123
Bone spurs, 5, 6
Braces, 25
Breathing, relaxed, 82
Bursae, 3, **186**
Bursitis, 13

C

C-reactive protein test, 9
Calcium and osteoporosis, 70–71
Canes, 25–28
Car trips, 159–160
Cardiovascular health, 29–30
Career changes, 82, 170, 172–178.
  See also Workplace issues
Carpal tunnel syndrome, 170
Cartilage, **186**
  and arthritis, 4, 6–7
  arthroscopic debridement, 122
  in knee replacement, 130
  transplantation, 151
Cementless implants, 124, 126, 128, 130–131
Chair exercises, 32–33

Chiropractors, 141
Chondroitin, 139
Chronic pain, 57–58
Clinical trials, 145
Cold treatments, 52
Collagen, **186**
Complement system, **186**
Complementary medicine, 135–146
Computed tomography (CT), **186**
Computer use, 169–170
Contrast baths, 54
Cooking tips, 64–65
Copper bracelets, 138
Corticosteroids
    drug interactions, 97–98
    general information, 92
    long-term therapy, 95
    short-term therapy, 94–95
    side effects, 96–97
    when needed, 93–94
Cortisol, 92
COX (cyclooxygenase), 91, **187**
COX-2 inhibitors, 90–92, 115
Cranial arteritis, 13
Cyst, **187**
Cytokines, 108, 111, 148, **187**

D

Deep breathing, 82
Degenerative arthritis. *See* Osteoarthritis
Depression, 75, 77, 83
Diathermy, 56
Dietary recommendations, 60–63
DMARDs (disease-modifying
    antirheumatic drugs), 95, 98–102,
    116–117
DMSO (dimethyl sulfoxide), 138
Door handles, 26
Dressing aids, 22, 24
Drugs. *See* Medications

E

Eburnation, 7
Elastin, **187**
Elbow surgery, 126
Electric heating pads, 53
Employment issues. *See* Workplace
    issues
Endothelium, **187**
Enthesis, **187**
Epidemiology, **187**
Equipment suppliers, 28
Erythrocyte sedimentation rate, 9
Estrogen replacement therapy, 70, 150
Exercise
    activity goals, 32, 38–39, 69
    aerobic, 29–30, 50
    aquatic, 33
    benefits, 17, 29–30
    for flexibility, 40–46
    joint protection guidelines, 18–21
    low-impact vs. high-impact, 32
    organized programs, 32–34
    and osteoarthritis, 152
    and osteoporosis, 30, 70
    and pain, 18–19, 30, 38, 39, 54
    range-of-motion, 18, 38
    for strength, 36, 46–50
    for travelers, 159
    using weights, 39
    videos, 34
    walking, 31, 40

F

Fat intake, 62
Fatigue, 21–22, 30
Fibromyalgia, 14–15
Finger joints, 5, 6, 7, 125
Fish oils, 68, 142
Fitness, 34–37
Flare-ups, 10, 21
Flexibility exercises, 40–46

Food and drug interactions, 71–72
Foot surgery, 131
Frozen shoulder, **187**
Fruits, 60–61

G

Gel packs, 53
Genetic factors, 2, 150–151
Giant cell arteritis, 13
Glucocorticoids, **187**
Glucosamine, 139
Gold rings, 139
Gold therapy, 99–100, 116
Gonorrhea, 14
Gout, 12
Grip size, 23, 27
Grooming aids, 23
Guided imagery, 79, 139–140

H

Half-life of medications, 93
Hand surgery, 125
Heat treatments, 53–54, 56
Heberden's nodes, 5, **187**
Hepatitis B, 14
Herbal treatments, 140
Hip surgery, 127–128
Homeopathic treatments, 140–141
Housecleaning tips, 25
Human leukocyte antigens (HLA), **188**
Hyaluronic acid, **188**
Hypnosis, 80, 141

I

Ice massage, 52
Ice packs, 52
Icy Hot, 112
Immune complex, **188**
Immune system, 7, 73–74, 102, **188**
Immunoglobulins, **188**
Immunosuppressants, 102–108, 117–118

Inflammation, 7, 86, 91, 108
International travel, 160, 162
Internet health information, 180–181

J

Jar openers, 22
Job issues. *See* Workplace issues
Joint fusion, 123
Joint manipulations, 141
Joint prostheses. *See* Total joint
    replacement
Joint protection
    assistive devices, 22–28, 167, 178
    exercise and rest, 18–21
    at work, 167–168
Joint replacement. *See* Total joint
    replacement
Joints, 3, 124, 130, 131, **188**
Journal keeping, 80–81

K

Kitchen helpers, 22, 24–25, 64–65
Knee surgery, 128, 130–131

L

Laminectomy, **188**
Leukocytes, **188**
Lifestyle changes, 63–67, 81–82
Ligament surgery, 123
Ligaments, 3, **189**
Low-impact activities, 32
Luggage, 26
Lupus erythematosus, 11
Lyme disease, 14
Lymphocyte, **189**

M

Magnet therapy, 141–142
Magnetic resonance imaging (MRI), **189**
Massage therapy, 54, 56, 80

Mayo Clinic Health Information
Web site, 120, 180
Mayo Clinic Health Letter, 180
Mayo Clinic Healthy Weight Pyramid,
60–63
Mayo Clinic Women's HealthSource, 180
Medical equipment suppliers, 28
Medicare coverage
canes, 28
TENS, 56
Medication usage
appetite effects, 72
drug absorption, 105
drug allergies, 101
drug interactions, 97
drug reactions, 104
generic vs. brand-name, 88
half-life, 93
interactions with food, 71–72
reasons for use, 85–86
side effects, 101
Medications
acetaminophen, 111
Actonel (risedronate), 71
Actron (ketoprofen), 115
Advil (ibuprofen), 88, 115
alendronate, 71
Aleve (naproxen sodium), 88, 115
allopurinol, 105
alprazolam, 114
Amigisic (salsalate), 115
amitriptyline, 113
anakinra, 99, 108, 111, 118
analgesics, 88, 110, 111–112, 119
Anaprox (naproxen sodium), 115
Ansaid (flurbiprofen), 89, 115
anti-inflammatory drugs, 86–98,
115–116
anti-TNF drugs, 108–110, 148
antidepressant drugs, 113
Arava (leflunomide), 103, 107–108, 118
Aristocort (triamcinolone), 96, 116
Arthricare Double Ice, 112
Arthrotec, 89, 115

Ascriptin (aspirin), 115
Aspercreme, 112
aspirin, 87–88, 111, 115
Aventyl (nortriptyline), 113
azathioprine, 102, 105, 117, 132
Azulfidine (sulfasalazine), 99, 100–101,
116
Bayer (aspirin), 88, 115
Bextra (valdecoxib), 91, 115
Bufferin (aspirin), 88, 115
calcitonin, 70–71
Capzasin-P (capsaicin), 112
carisoprodol, 113
Cataflam (diclofenac), 115
Celebrex (celecoxib), 91, 115
chlordiazepoxide, 114
choline magnesium trisalicylate, 90, 115
Clinoril (sulindac), 89, 115
codeine, 112, 119
Codone (hydrocodone), 119
corticosteroids, 92–98
cortisone, 56, 93, 96, 116
Cortone Acetate (cortisone), 96, 116
Cuprimine (penicillamine), 102
cyclobenzaprine, 113
cyclophosphamide, 102, 106–107, 117
cyclosporine, 103, 106, 117, 132
Cytoxan (cyclophosphamide), 102,
106, 117
Darvon-N (propoxyphene), 112, 119
Daypro (oxaprozin), 115
Deltasone (prednisone), 96, 116
Demerol (meperidine), 112, 119
Depen (penicillamine), 102
desipramine, 113
Desyrel (trazodone), 113
diazepam, 114
diclofenac sodium, 89, 115
diflunisal, 115
Disalcid (salsalate), 90, 115
DMARDs, 95, 98–102, 116–117
Dolobid (diflunisal), 115
Elavil (amitriptyline), 113
Enbrel (etanercept), 108–109, 118

Endep (amitriptyline), 113
etanercept, 99, 108–109, 118
etodolac, 89, 115
Eucalyptamint, 112
Evista (raloxifene), 70
Feldene (piroxicam), 89, 93, 115
fenoprofen, 89, 115
Flexeril (cyclobenzaprine), 113
flurbiprofen, 89, 115
Fosamax (alendronate), 71
gold, 99–100, 116
Hyalgan (hyaluronate), 114
hydrocodone, 112, 119
hydroxychloroquine, 99, 116
hylan G-F 20, 114
ibuprofen, 88, 115
imipramine, 113
immunosuppressants, 102–108,
    117–118
Imuran (azathioprine), 102, 105, 117, 132
Indocin (indomethacin), 89, 115
infliximab, 99, 108, 110, 118
ketoprofen, 88, 115
Kineret (anakinra), 108, 111, 118
leflunomide, 103, 107–108, 118
Librium (chlordiazepoxide), 114
Lodine (etodolac), 89, 115
Medrol (methylprednisolone), 96, 116
meloxicam, 89, 115
meperidine, 112, 119
methotrexate, 103–104, 117, 132
methylprednisolone, 96, 116
Miacalcin (calcitonin), 70–71
Minocin (minocycline), 99, 102, 117
minocycline, 99, 102, 117, 149
misoprostol, 89, 115
Mobic (meloxicam), 89, 115
Motrin IB (ibuprofen), 88, 115
muscle relaxants, 113
Myochrysine (gold), 99–100, 116
nabumetone, 89, 115
Nalfon (fenoprofen), 89, 115
Naprelan (naproxen), 89, 115
Naprosyn (naproxen), 89, 115

naproxen sodium, 88, 115
narcotics, 112, 119
Neoral (cyclosporine), 103, 106, 117, 132
nonacetylated salicylates, 90
Norpramin (desipramine), 113
nortriptyline, 113
NSAIDs, 86–90, 115
Nuprin (ibuprofen), 115
Orasone (prednisone), 96, 116
Orudis KT (ketoprofen), 88, 115
Oruvail (ketoprofen), 115
oxaprozin, 115
OxyContin (oxycodone), 112
Pamelor (nortriptyline), 113
penicillamine, 102
piroxicam, 89, 93, 115
Plaquenil (hydroxychloroquine), 99, 116
prednisolone, 96, 116
prednisone, 96, 116
Prelone (prednisolone), 96, 116
propoxyphene, 112, 119
raloxifene, 70
Relafen (nabumetone), 89, 115
Remicade (infliximab), 108, 110, 118
Rheumatrex (methotrexate), 103–104,
    117
Ridaura (gold), 116
risedronate, 71
rofecoxib, 91, 115
salsalate, 90, 115
Sandimmune (cyclosporine), 103, 117,
    132
sertraline, 113
Solganal (gold), 99–100, 116
Soma (carisoprodol), 113
Sportscreme, 112
Sterapred (prednisone), 116
sulfasalazine, 99, 100–101, 116
sulindac, 89, 115
Synvisc (hylan G-F 20), 114
Tofranil (imipramine), 113
Tolectin (tolmetin), 89, 115
tramadol, 112, 119
trazodone, 113

triamcinolone, 96, 116
Trilisate (choline magnesium trisalicylate), 90, 115
Tylenol (acetaminophen), 111
Ultram (tramadol), 112, 119
valdecoxib, 91, 115
Valium (diazepam), 114
Vioxx (rofecoxib), 91, 115
Voltaren (diclofenac sodium), 89, 115
Xanax (alprazolam), 114
Zoloft (sertraline), 113
Zostrix (capsaicin), 112
Meditation, 79, 142
Menu planning, 63–64
Mind-body connection, 73–84
Mumps, 14
Muscle relaxants, 113
Muscular fitness, 34–36, 37
Myopathy, **189**

N

Narcotics, 112, 119
National Center for Complementary and Alternative Medicine, 145, 146
Negative thinking, 73, 76–77
Nerve blocks, 56
Neuropathy, **189**
NSAIDs (non-steroidal anti-inflammatory drugs), 86–90, 115
Nutrition
  calcium sources, 71
  evaluating claims, 71–72
  improving convenience foods, 64
  Mayo Clinic Healthy Weight Pyramid, 60–63
  menu planning, 63–64
  serving sizes, 62–63, 63, 66
Nutritional supplements, 142–143

O

Obesity and arthritis, 19, 68
Occupational therapists, 170, **189**

Omega-3 fatty acids, 68, 142
Optimism, 73–74
Orthopedic surgeons, 121
Osteoarthritis. *See also* Medications; Pain; Surgery
  cortisone injections, 93
  and exercise, 152
  and extra pounds, 19, 68, 152
  general information, 4–6
  hyaluronate injections, 114
  and inflammation, 86
Osteomyelitis, **189**
Osteopaths, 141
Osteophytes (bone spurs), 5
Osteoporosis, 15, 30, 70–71, **189**
Osteotomy, 122–123, 127, 128

P

Pain
  acupuncture, 136–137
  analgesics, 88, 111–112, 119
  biofeedback, 57, 138
  chronic pain centers, 58
  cold treatments, 52
  contrast baths, 54
  COX-2 inhibitors, 90–92, 115
  and exercise, 18–19, 30, 38, 54
  heat treatments, 53–54, 56
  and inflammation, 86
  massage, 54, 56, 80
  nerve blocks, 56
  psychological control, 57–58
  relaxation techniques, 57–58, 77, 79–80
  steroid injections, 56
  TENS, 56
  topical pain relievers, 112
Paraffin baths, 56
Periosteal transplantation, 151
Pessimism, 73
Physiatrist, **189**
Physical therapists, **189**
Placebo effect, 144
Polyarteritis nodosa, 13
Polymyalgia rheumatica, 13

Polymyositis, 12
Positive thinking, 73–74, 76–77
Posture, 37
Progressive muscle relaxation, 57–58, 79–80
Prosorba column, 109
Protein intake, 61–62
Pseudogout, 12
Psoriatic arthritis, 12
Psychoneuroimmunology, 74–75

Q

Quack treatments, 182–184

R

Range-of-motion exercises, 18, 38
Raynaud's phenomenon, 11
Reactive arthritis (Reiter's syndrome), 12
Reflex sympathetic dystrophy, **190**
Rehabilitation, postoperative, 133
Reiter's syndrome, 12
Relaxation techniques, 57–58, 77, 79–80, 82
Research, 145, 147–152
Resection (bone), 123
Resources
  Arthritis Foundation, 84, 179–180
  books, 84, 159, 182
  Internet health information, 120, 180–181
  job hunting, 177
  Mayo Clinic Health Information web site, 120, 180
  medical equipment suppliers, 28
  travel planning, 156, 162–164
  workplace issues, 178
Rest, 21–22, 83
Restaurants, 65–67
Rheumatic fever, **190**
Rheumatoid arthritis. *See also* Medications; Pain; Surgery
  and extra pounds, 68
  fatigue, 21–22, 30
  general information, 7–10
  genetic factors, 2, 150–151
  sleep requirements, 22
  tests for, 9–10
Rheumatoid factor test, 9
Rheumatoid nodules, 9
Rheumatologist, **190**
Ring splints, 22
Rotator cuff, **190**

S

SAMe (s-adenosyl methionine), 143
Scleroderma, 11
Sed rate. *See* Erythrocyte sedimentation rate
Self-efficacy, 83
Self-hypnosis, 80
Serving sizes, 62–63, 63, 66
Shoulder surgery, 126
Side effects of drugs, 101
Simplifying your life, 81–82
Sjogren's syndrome, 11
Sleep requirements, 22, 83
Snake venom, 143
Social support, 81
Soybean oil, 142–143
Spinal stenosis, 5
Spine
  ankylosing spondylitis, 12
  joint fusion, 123
  osteoarthritis, 6
Spondylarthropathy, 12
Staphylococcal infections, 13–14
Steroids, 56, 92. *See also* Corticosteroids
Strength exercises, 36, 46–50
Stress, 74–76, 79–80
Stretching, 18, 34–35
Support groups, 81
Surgery. *See also under specific joints*
  arthroplasty, 123
  arthroscopic debridement, 122
  arthroscopic synovectomy, 128, 151

autologous transfusion, 132
cartilage transplantation, 151
choosing a surgeon, 121–122
complications, 132
hospital stay, 133
joint fusion, 123
osteotomy, 122–123
periosteal transplantation, 151
preparing for, 131–132
recovery, 134
rehabilitation, 133
replacement arthroplasty, 123
resection, 123
risks, 132
second opinions, 122
synovectomy, 122
tendons and ligaments, 123
Syndesmophytes, **190**
Synovectomy, 122, 151, **190**
Synovial fluid, 3, 114, **190**
Synovial membrane, 3, **190**
inflammation, 7–8
synovectomy, 122, 151
Systemic lupus erythematosus, 11

T

Tai Chi, 33–34, 35
Temporal arteritis, 13
Tendinitis, 13
Tendon surgery, 123, 125, 131
Tendons, 3, **190**
TENS (transcutaneous electrical nerve stimulation), 56
Tests
    fitness, 36–37
    for rheumatoid arthritis, 9–10
Thunder god vine (Tripterygium wilfordii), 140
TNF (tumor necrosis factor), 108
Tophus, **190**
Total joint replacement, 123
    ankles and feet, 131

elbow, 126
hand and wrist, 125
hip, 127–128, 134
implant failures, 126, 132
implant wear, 124, 132
knee, 130–131, 134
shoulder, 126
TPMT gene, 104
Tranquilizers, 114
Transcendental meditation, 79
Traveling with arthritis, 153–164
Tuberculous arthritis, 14

U

Ultrasound heat therapy, 56

V

Vaccines, 149
Vegetables, 60
Visualization, 79, 139–140
Vitamin D and calcium, 70
Vitamins and arthritis, 142, 152

W

Walking assistance. *See* Canes
Walking for exercise, 31
Warming up, 18, 38
Water exercise, 33
Weight control, 19, 62–63, 68–69, 152
Weights and exercise, 39
Workplace issues, 165–178
World Wide Web health information, 180–181
Wrist surgery, 125
Writing, 26

X

X-rays
    and osteoarthritis, 7
    and rheumatoid arthritis, 9–10

MAYO CLINIC ON HEALTH

Alzheimer's Disease

Arthritis

Chronic Pain

Depression

Digestive Health

Healthy Aging

Healthy Weight

Hearing

High Blood Pressure

Managing Diabetes

Osteoporosis

Prostate Health

Vision and Eye Health

Additional Health titles from **Mason Crest Publishers**

COMPACT GUIDES TO FITNESS AND HEALTH

Alternative Medicine and Your Health
Eating Out: Your Guide to Healthy Dining
Everyday Fitness: Look Good, Feel Good
Getting the Most from Your Medications
Healthy Meals for Hurried Lives
Healthy Traveler
Healthy Weight for Life
Heart Healthy Eating Guide for Women
Live Longer, Live Better
Living Disease-Free
Medical Tests Every Man Needs
Stretching Your Health Care Dollar
Your Guide to Vitamin & Mineral Supplements
Your Healthy Back
8 Ways to Lower Your Risk of a Heart Attack or Stroke
10 Tips for Better Hearing
20 Tasty Recipes for People with Diabetes